Jon Scieszka presents

GUYS WRITE FOR
GUYS
READ

VIKING

VIKING
Published by Penguin Group
Penguin Young Readers Group, 345 Hudson Street, New York, New York 10014, U.S.A.
Penguin Group (Canada), 90 Eglinton Avenue East, Suite 700, Toronto, Ontario, Canada M4P 2Y3
(a division of Pearson Penguin Canada Inc.)
Penguin Books Ltd, 80 Strand, London WC2R 0RL, England
Penguin Ireland, 25 St Stephen's Green, Dublin 2, Ireland (a division of Penguin Books Ltd)
Penguin Group (Australia), 250 Camberwell Road, Camberwell, Victoria 3124, Australia
(a division of Pearson Australia Group Pty Ltd)
Penguin Books India Pvt Ltd, 11 Community Centre, Panchsheel Park, New Delhi - 110 017, India
Penguin Group (NZ), 67 Apollo Drive, Rosedale, North Shore 0632, New Zealand
(a division of Pearson New Zealand Ltd.)
Penguin Books (South Africa) (Pty) Ltd, 24 Sturdee Avenue, Rosebank, Johannesburg 2196, South Africa

Penguin Books Ltd, Registered Offices: 80 Strand, London WC2R 0RL, England

First published in 2005 by Viking, a division of Penguin Young Readers Group
This edition published in 2008 by Viking, a division of Penguin Young Readers Group

3   5   7   9   10   8   6   4   2

THE LIBRARY OF CONGRESS HAS CATALOGED THE PREVIOUS VIKING EDITION AS FOLLOWS:
Guys write for guys read / Jon Scieszka (editor).
p. cm.
ISBN 978-0-670-06007-0 (hardcover)
1. Men—Literary Collections. 2. American Literature—Male authors. 3. Children's literature, American.
I. Scieszka, Jon
PS509.M46G89 2005   810.8'09286-dc22   2004028984

This edition ISBN 978-0-670-01144-5 (paperback)

This book is set in Goudy   Book design by Jim Hoover   Printed in the U.S.A.

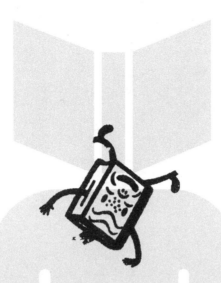

★ CONTENTS ★

Illustrator pieces are indicated with a star

FOREWORD

Now here is some writing for guys.

You are holding in your hands ninety-two pieces of work from a crazy variety of writers and illustrators—all about being a guy.

Inside this book are their stories, memories, comic strips, poems, drawings done when they were kids, advice, schemes, jokes, and dreams. They are funny, action-packed, sad, goofy, gross, touching, stupid, true—and all very short.

I asked each of these guys to donate something so I could use the money from the book to build a Web site to help boys read.

They did (give something).

And I did (build the guysread.com Web site).

Because the problem is that there are a lot of boys who are not all that crazy about reading. Kids know this. Parents know this. Teachers and librarians know this. National statistics for the last twenty-five years show this. But we need to do something to change this. So the basic idea of *Guys Read* is to help get boys interested in reading by connecting them with things they will want to read.

All these guys know what boys like to read. Most of the writers and illustrators were suggested by voters at the original *Guys Read* Web site. There are also newspaper writers, magazine editors and writers, and professors included because they care about boys and their reading. So go check out a few pieces. See if you find something you like. You can find other work by these guys in the bibliography after each piece. And check out the *Guys Read* Web site at www.guysread.com for more recommendations, information about guys and reading, and links to authors and illustrators.

Huge thanks to all of the guys in this anthology for helping out.

I had so much fun writing my contribution to the first edition of this collection that I decided to write a whole book about growing up with my five crazy brothers. The new book is called *Knucklehead: Tall Tales and Mostly True Stories about Growing Up Scieszka.* As an extra thanks to all of you supporters of *Guys Read,* I've added one of my *Knucklehead* pieces to this new edition. It's called "Roommates."

Enjoy it . . . and any and all of the knucklehead guys in your life.

Jon Scieszka
Brooklyn, N.Y., 2008

JON SCIESZKA

Roommates (excerpt from Knucklehead)

Since there were six boys, it worked out just right that everyone had a roommate: Jim and Jon, Tom and Gregg, Brian and Jeff.

It worked out pretty well for me because Jim was neat and not too much of a pain in the neck like the little brothers. But man, could Jim talk.

I think Jim knew from the time he was four that he was going to be a lawyer. He was always trying to win an argument or make a case why you should agree with him. Jim would talk and talk, and then talk some more.

His best pitch ever was the time he tried to sell me my own shirt.

I was looking for a clean shirt to wear. Most of my clothes were in a pile on the floor of my closet. I was digging through the pile, sniffing for one that was not too smelly.

Jim pulled a clean, folded, short-sleeved shirt out of his dresser drawer.

"I really should save this shirt, Jon. But because you need it, I'm going to give you a deal," said Jim.

I found a shirt with only a couple of grass stains on the elbows.

"What's that?" I said.

"This is an excellent shirt, a clean shirt, a lightweight shirt, a short-sleeved shirt," said Jim. "But because you need it, I'm going to give it to you for a bargain price."

I held up a pretty good-looking dark blue shirt. It smelled like the two-week-old socks still hanging on it.

"Look at this shirt. It's a great shirt. Probably the best shirt," said Jim. "And I am going to let you have it, while I wear my same old shirt, for only fifty cents."

I looked at the shirt. It was a great shirt.

"It's perfectly clean," said Jim.

He was right. It was perfectly clean.

I checked my pockets.

"I've only got twenty-five cents," I said.

Jim put the shirt back in his drawer.

"I'm afraid I can't go any lower than forty cents. It's my only clean shirt. I'm going to need it soon. I was going to do you a favor, but I can see it's not going to work out."

I tried on a brown shirt. It smelled even worse than the green shirt.

"Maybe I can get twenty-five cents off Tom," I said. "Let me see the shirt."

Jim handed it over. I tried it on. It fit perfectly. It was clean. It was so . . . familiar.

"Hey," I said. "This is my shirt."

"It was in my drawer," said Jim. "You owe me fifty cents."

"I do not."

"You do too."

"Do not."

"Take it off."

"Make me."

Our legal debate quickly turned into a wrestling match. Jim jumped on me. I got him in a headlock. We rolled around on our bedroom floor. And I think I made Jim a better, stronger lawyer.

LLOYD ALEXANDER
The Truth about the World

My first date never happened. When I finally built up enough nerve, I dared to ask one of the girls in my ninth-grade class to go to some kind of dance or other—I don't remember exactly; it was long ago. To my amazement, she accepted. For myself, I always thought in large, long-range terms. We would, I imagined, become sweethearts, get engaged, eventually marry, and live happily ever after.

Friday afternoon, the day before the glorious event, our gym teacher ordered us outdoors to play soccer. I usually preferred loitering around the fringes of the action, but when the ball bounded straight at me, I seized the moment to give it the mightiest kick in school history.

I noticed a couple of things. For one, I glimpsed the ball rocketing across the field, missing the goal by what looked like about half a mile; for another, I saw an expression of despondency and long suffering on the face of the gym teacher. By then, I was on the grass, trying to hold my left foot in both hands and giving my full attention to learning the nature of agony.

A couple of classmates hauled me to the nurse's office. My mother had to be summoned. She took me home in our ancient Plymouth and phoned the doctor (they made house calls in those days). He examined my foot, now swollen to the size of a baked ham. He assured me I would live. I was sorry to hear that.

The date, of course, was off. My mother took charge of cancelling it; I hadn't the heart to do it myself. In those days, pain was supposed to build character. After nearly a week of character-building, I limped back to school. I was too ashamed even to look at my might-have-been date. And she, very properly, decided the right thing to do was never to speak to me again. Worse, some treacherous classmates spread the false rumor that I had gotten scared of actually dating a girl and faked the whole incident.

There is always a bright side. The incident taught me the truth about the world. It is not a good place. Life is ruled by unfair and malicious fate, filled with injustice, humiliation, shame, despair, tears and woe, misery undiluted. Naturally, I became a writer. I didn't know how to dance, anyway.

Biography:

Grew up: Philadelphia, Pennsylvania

Now lives: Drexel Hill, Pennsylvania

Random fact: Sleeps when he can't write (he calls it "thinking horizontally")

Selected Bibliography:

The Book of Three (Chronicles of Prydain #1)

The Black Cauldron (Chronicles of Prydain #2)

The Castle of Llyr (Chronicles of Prydain #3)

M. T. ANDERSON
My Maturity, in Flames

Not far from where I live now, there is a town where ancient houses stand around a quiet green, a town with views that sweep all the way from Massachusetts to the mountains of Vermont and New Hampshire. A friend of mine lived there, and once, when she and her parents were going to be away for several weeks, they asked me whether I could live in their house for them while they were gone and make sure it weathered the snow.

I was perhaps seventeen. I had never lived alone. This was exciting. They were gone, and the house was mine. I walked in the front door and spread my arms out. The windows looked out over a landscape of pines and ice. I felt that I was master of all I surveyed.

I have always been somewhat of an incompetent, so I was determined to get this right. For two weeks, I treated that house gingerly, lovingly. I watered the geraniums. I washed all the dishes by hand. I avoided making any impression on the cushions. I didn't move anything, not even the baleful, curly-haired china doll that they left, for some ungodly reason, glaring down the steps at me from the attic, just waiting for me to go to sleep so it could sink its little porcelain fangs into my hamstrings.

Occasionally, I would drop cheerful little notes to my friend's parents, saying things like, "Don't worry about a thing. Everything's fine here. Incidentally, would you call the brick wall in the living room a 'structural' wall? Just wondering. Hope to hear from you soon! —MTA."

At the end of the two weeks, I was startled to discover that I had behaved responsibly the whole time. I hadn't blown it. Nothing was broken.

I cleaned the place up and prepared to leave. Knowing that I have a tendency to worry—I had once, when twelve, alerted a whole London neighborhood to the presence of an asthmatic serial killer who turned out to be a loose awning—I double-checked everything that could possibly go wrong in the house. The basement was dry. All of the burners on the stove were off. The back door was locked. I loaded my car and prepared to drive away.

Suddenly, it occurred to me that I hadn't checked the iron. I got out of the car, unlocked the front door, ran upstairs, and checked the iron. It was off. I ran downstairs, shut the front door, got in the car, looked at the front door, got out of the car, went to the front door, rattled the front door to make sure it was locked, got back into the car, and drove away.

I had only gone a mile or two when I began to feel like something was wrong. The iron. Sometimes it is not clear if you have checked a heating element *enough*.

I should perhaps mention at this point that I had never used the iron while at the house. I had never touched it before I checked it. This made it unlikely that the iron was on.

But some irons are actually activated by movement. When you pick them up, they turn on. Maybe checking the iron had been the very thing that caused it to heat up.

This was patently ridiculous. Thinking back, I dimly remembered actually unplugging the iron when I checked it. At least, upon reflection, I thought I remembered unplugging it. I drove on.

Resolutely, I decided that, as I had never used the iron, if it was on, it was not my fault. The iron would have to have been on since the family left two weeks ago. If the house burned down, it was technically their fault.

But they wouldn't know that. They would think I had left the iron on. They would hate me. They would walk through the blackened ruins of their beautiful home and hiss my name.

But I had checked the iron. I was almost entirely sure that it hadn't been on. Unless it came on from jiggling. In the way that some do. I thought.

I was now a half an hour away from the house. I could still call the next-door neighbors and ask them to check. But that would blow my cool. "Could you break into the house next door and see if I left the iron on . . . which I never used?"

No, I thought. *I will be an adult. I will not cave in to this fantasy.*

I turned on the radio to something soothing. The slow movement of a Mozart piano concerto. *This,* I thought, *is what adults listen to, instead of the raving paranoiac voices within them.*

It was a big mistake. Because it turns out that the slow movement of a Mozart piano concerto—with all its lilt and elegance—is, to someone in my state, precisely the soundtrack for disaster. It is just the kind of pleasant, polite music you hear in a movie when someone is smiling to himself, driving away from a house where he has stayed for two weeks, and then you cut to the iron setting fire to the ironing board cover. Then you flash back to the kid in the car, contented, tapping time to the Mozart, and then back to the flaming curtains, then back to the kid going down the highway, waving at some toddlers in the back of a minivan, then back to the house completely in flames, the fire department kicking in the door, screaming, timbers falling; and, just as the slow movement of the Mozart piano concerto ends, a shot of the glowing embers, with the china doll smiling up out of the ruins.

I stopped at a gas station. I called the neighbors. They weren't home. I begged their answering machine to go check the iron. I blathered to the answering machine that I hadn't used the iron, but that maybe instead of turning it off when I checked it, I had turned it on—I asked the neighbors this and many more favors—and I hoped that during adulthood, things would be different, that things would be sure and safe—the irons upright, the Mozart calm, the doll, at long last, entombed inside a trunk—that things, by then, would not always be on fire.

Oh well.

Biography:

Grew up: Stow, Massachusetts

Now lives: Boston, Massachusetts

Random fact: Just came back from a month-long trip to China; went into the desert to search for the Temple of the Rat-King . . . and found it. Was also stuffed in a ceramic vat and juggled on the feet of a Chinese giantess.

Selected Bibliography:

Feed

The Game of Sunken Places

Burger Wuss

DANIEL ADEL

Daniel Adel, 1968

My mom braved the very shaky pull-down ladder that leads to the attic to dig up this dusty gem from sometime in my elementary school days. I think it was an attempt at drawing myself giving a bouquet of flowers to my mom, but being a guy I couldn't bring myself to draw a bouquet of flowers (I still can't), so it sort of came out a bouquet of tree. Much more manly.

As my painting has "evolved," there's been a strong tendency for the heads to get progressively bigger as the hands shrink down to little claws. Finding this old drawing has helped me, for the moment anyhow, to correct this problem.

Some things never change. I'm still doing lots of drawings and paintings of people holding things: a film director holding a bellows fanning the flames under Nicole Kidman's feet, Jerry Seinfeld holding a small head of Jerry Seinfeld. On the other hand some things do change a bit. I'm sure I was listening to Pete Seeger singing folk songs when I drew the first picture, back in the early sixties, or maybe Herb Alpert and the Tijuana Brass playing the theme song from *The Dating Game*. The updated version was mostly done to the soothing sounds of German or Japanese industrial music like Farben, Stillupsteypa, and Skist. And a guy who makes music from the clicks and pops of a busted piece of electronic equipment that he dropped on the floor.

Which I guess is sort of like doing a painting based on an old buried scribble you dropped on the floor when you were a kid that your mom picked up and stashed away because she thought it might be useful someday.

I've searched in vain for the French influence on this piece, as it was painted here in the south of France. But apart from the fact that the fingers look a bit more like baguettes than fingers, I seem to have succeeded in coming all the way to France only to paint exactly the way I do when I'm in New York City. Oh well.

I can't explain the fez.

Biography:

Grew up: New Rochelle (once the home of Norman Rockwell) and Larchmont, New York

Now lives: Somewhere between Lacoste, France (once the home of the Marquis de Sade), and Larchmont, New York

Random fact: Would like his work to become a perfect combination of Norman Rockwell and the Marquis de Sade

Selected Bibliography:

The Book That Jack Wrote by Jon Scieszka

Daniel Adel, 2005

MARC ARONSON

Stone = Throw

When I was growing up in Manhattan, sports meant running out into Central Park, where depending on my age or the season, we played fungo games, running bases, touch football, softball, pick-up basketball, Wiffle ball—any combination of boys, equipment, and whatever fields we could mark with muddy jackets, rocks, and sticks. Sports was not an activity, it was a time period: Saturday, finish breakfast, run out to the field, see what happened. I realized around the time my son was born that the sports life of my childhood no longer existed in Manhattan. Central Park is a carefully patrolled grass museum, where the wealthy ladies who pay for the maintenance of the park put up endless fences and signs, warning that seeds are germinating and that you had best keep off. Great for grass, terrible for kids.

I can't say we left the city and moved to the suburbs because they ruined the park, but it helped. My son was two when we bought the house on a slight hill in Maplewood, a five-minute brisk walk from the train station. It was not long before he and I would amble down the hill to buy something or look at the trains go by. A walk with a two-year-old is very Zen; it is not

about the end but the journey. He needs to pet the dog someone is walking; to roll down the slight incline to the church
basement, and then roll again, and again, and again; to remind
me of the place where the wasps (he calls them bees) live, then
zoom past it.

Along the way, we pass by a driveway filled with gravel. From
the age where he could first walk, he needed to stop there, pick
up a stone, and throw it. Not to throw at something as a test of
aim—not to throw in anger as a protest—not even to see how far
it would go. It was simple: stone = throw.

Sasha's world is filled with those equations: fallen tree =
balance beam; puddle = splash; stick = gun = "I shoot you
dead"; shadow = "monsters, let's get them"; walk = race = "I'm
the winner."

No doubt my enjoyment of his physical, rambunctious
temperament and my willingness to shoot monsters and chase
imaginary bad guys with him encourages those sides of Sasha's
personality. But I did not teach him stone = throw. There is
something elemental in that. There is no goal, just an urgent
necessity, a compelling need. Dogs raise their legs to trees; boys
throw stones.

Sasha is left-handed and is now three. He's willing to spend
some time learning how a lefty holds a bat or catches with a
mitt or dribbles a soccer ball. His interest in acquiring skills
waxes and wanes. Throwing stones is not something he does to
sharpen his aim or to improve his ability to pitch. It is just a
demand that the landscape makes on his nervous system. Nice
small stones that fit easily in your hand are there to be picked
up, to be hefted a minute in the palm of your hand to sense
their weight, and to be tossed.

We have already started the soccer and tennis and swimming

lessons. My childhood of free play is as impossible here as it was in the city. But at least in the gravel in the driveway, Sasha gets a few minutes of being a pure boy: a being designed for picking up round objects and throwing them. And long may that pure physical joy reign as a boy's freedom, and a boy's delight.

Biography:

Grew up: Upper West Side of Manhattan
Now lives: Maplewood, New Jersey
Random fact: Once stole a pass in high school basketball at the old Madison Square Garden. Clearly remembers the steal and having the whole Garden court ahead of him. Is less clear about whether he made the layup at the other end.

Selected Bibliography:

Witch-Hunt: Mysteries of the Salem Witch Trials
Exploding the Myths: The Truth about Teenagers and Reading
Sir Walter Ralegh and the Quest for El Dorado

AVI

Superpatriot

Superman. Batman. Robin. Wonder Woman. The Flash. Hawkman. Plastic Man. The Green Lantern. Captain America. Captain Marvel Junior. Mary Marvel. Uncle Marvel. Best of all, Captain Marvel. To name only the important ones.

They may have been comic book characters to some people, but they were my role models. Hardly a coincidence that all these superheroes went through life pretending (like me) to be normal. With a quick change of costume (better than underwear) or, in the case of Billy Batson, at the utterance of a magic word—*Shazam!*—they turned into superheroes. They didn't just right the wrongs in the world; they always thought of other people. Not one selfish or self-serving bone in their muscular bodies. No wonder that, having worked hard to defeat our enemies during World War II, they were great patriots.

I never could read enough about them. But then I was aiming to be a superhero. After all, I had mastered half the role—being, like Clark Kent, mild mannered.

Then I learned the truth about myself.

It happened in 1946. Right after the war. I was nine years old.

Hospitals were full of wounded military personnel. Somehow I learned that they, too, liked comic books. As they convalesced, they would enjoy some.

I decided to hold a comic book drive at my school, Public School Eight. During the war, there were many such patriotic collection efforts. Newspapers. Scrap metal. Even string. So when I asked my teacher if I could organize a comic book collection drive for "our boys" in hospitals, I received an enthusiastic "OK."

To announce this drive, I went from class to class and spoke about how our boys had sacrificed a lot for us. How unselfish they were. That by giving them our beloved comics, we, too, could be unselfish patriots. I spoke at the weekly assembly, making a rousing patriotic speech. I was praised. My parents were praised. And the comic books came pouring in.

Hundreds of them. Sure, there were some Little Lulus, and Archies—girl comic books—but so what? I read each and every one of them. I read them in the morning before school. After school. At night. I read them under the covers. In the bathtub. At the dinner table. On the toilet.

"Don't you think you should send them off to the hospitals?" my mother prodded. She had found a place to send them—along with an address and a willingness to pay the postage.

"I haven't finished reading them all," I said.

"Who are they for?" she asked.

I was too busy reading to answer.

A month later, I came home from school and discovered she had scooped them up, packaged them, and sent them off.

I was mad. "They were mine!" I protested.

"Oh?" she replied, with a lift of one eyebrow.

A few weeks later I received a letter from the hospital. They thanked me lavishly. Told me how much the boys enjoyed the gift. The last line read, "America is great because of unselfish patriots like you."

Soon as I read that line, I knew—as sure as I knew anything—that my motives had not been pure. I wanted to read those comic books myself. I had been selfish. I was not going to be a superhero.

Oh, I kept on reading about superheroes. But I was reading about them, not me. It was clear even to me that I was doomed to remain just . . . mild mannered.

Biography:
Grew up: Brooklyn, New York
Now lives: Denver, Colorado
Random fact: Wrote the comic book *City of Light, City of Dark*

Selected Bibliography
Nothing but the Truth: A Documentary Novel
Poppy illustrated by Brian Floca
Windcatcher

T. A. BARRON

The Crossing

There it was: the deepest gorge I'd ever seen.

Like a bottomless gash in the mountainside, this gorge opened under the waterfall that had poured here relentlessly, season after season, century after century. Water slammed down into it, smashing the granite cliff walls, thundering like a thousand storms. Mist exploded upward, rising and billowing into the sky.

I stood there, watching, leaning against a mossy boulder. "The crossing." That was what the ancient Anasazi name for this gorge meant. Was there something special about those cliff walls on the other side? And if not, why would the Anasazi have ever tried to cross over that churning, crashing death trap?

I bit through the straw I was chewing. *One way to find out, right?*

Carefully, I stepped over the slippery, spray-soaked rocks to the edge of the chasm. Pulling off my backpack, I hooked my foot through one of the straps so that the pack's weight would hold me back. Carefully, very carefully, I leaned over into the gorge.

A blast of water slapped my face, cold as the icy glaciers up on the summit! I pulled back and wiped my face. Anyone crazy enough to try to cross at this spot, who didn't die from the fall alone, would surely die from the chill of landing in water that cold.

How many people before me had actually died right here?

Perhaps "the crossing" meant the passage from life into death? Only the Anasazi knew the answer, and they had vanished without a trace hundreds of years before.

Oh well, guess I'd rather stay alive. So I won't find out after all.

I grabbed my pack and hoisted it onto my back. As I slipped my arm through the strap, brushing against my fly rod, I thought of the rainbow trout I was hoping to catch for supper. Rainbow, freshly caught and cooked over a fire with plenty of butter and chili peppers, was the best mountain meal of all. I licked my lips and turned to go, glad to be alive.

That was when something seemed to grab my shoulder and tug me toward the gorge. My boots slipped on the rocks and I lurched over backward. Whatever scream I let loose was swallowed completely in the roaring, pounding cascade.

The last thing I remember was how, as I plummeted into the chasm, the colors around me suddenly shifted. Mist rose up around me, like a new landscape being born. For an instant, I thought that maybe I wasn't really dying after all. Just changing.

Or perhaps . . . crossing into somewhere else. Somewhere beyond the world I'd always known.

The world I'd left behind.

Biography:

Grew up: On a ranch near Pike's Peak, Colorado

Now lives: On a farm, with wife Currie and five kids, near Long's Peak, Colorado

Random fact: Has never met a dangerous river crossing that he didn't like . . . even if he fell in

Selected Bibliography:

The Fires of Merlin (The Lost Years of Merlin epic #3)

The Mirror of Merlin (The Lost Years of Merlin epic #4)

The Wings of Merlin (The Lost Years of Merlin epic #5)

TEDD ARNOLD
Reading Can Be Dangerous

Yes, dangerous. It's true. Like when you read that history assignment on the way to school while riding your bike. Or when you get lost in a book and don't know what's going on around you—like when you're all wrapped up in the exciting last chapter of *Skateboard Monkey* and a shadow falls across the page and you realize your teacher is standing there waiting for you to answer the question she asked you at least a half hour ago and your whole class is grinning at you, eager to witness your doom.

What happened to me wasn't *that* bad. But I still remember one of the times I got lost in a book, back when I was a teenager. I was, along with lots of other guys, reading every James Bond spy novel I could get my hands on. (We're talking 1960s, if you must know.) One day I was home alone, enjoying my favorite food—a heaping plate of leftover spaghetti and meatballs. And I was reading. No, I wasn't just reading. I was gripped, absorbed, like, not even in the building anymore—totally checked out—lost in a cool James Bond book.

My family had this pet bird, a big white cockatoo named Luke. He mostly hung out on a perch just inside our sliding glass patio doors, but he was free to fly around in the house. Luke couldn't talk like some trained birds, but that didn't stop

him from chatting with people. His talk sounded like chuckling.

So, I'm at the table eating and reading, and Luke's talking to me, and I'm not paying any attention. I don't hear him. I don't see him. I don't know anything that isn't on the plate or on the page in front of me.

Oh, did I mention? Luke lo-o-o-o-oved spaghetti.

Somewhere in his little bird brain, Luke must have decided I wasn't being sensitive to his feelings. He took matters into his own hands, er, feet. He flew from his perch, swooped over the top of my book, and landed right on my spaghetti and meatballs.

I didn't mean to hurt him, I swear! But I didn't have time to think. My first reaction was the same that yours would be. I knocked him off my food with the back of my hand.

Luke's first reaction was to hold on to whatever he could. He clutched at my spaghetti with both feet. He went backwards head over heels and the spaghetti he grabbed went flying. Up the front of my shirt. Up my face. Up the wall behind me. Somehow, red sauce even splattered the ceiling.

Luke staggered to his feet and flew back to the perch, his butt feathers dripping spaghetti sauce all the way. He wasn't hurt, except for his dignity—but the sauce on his beautiful white plumage turned him splotchy orange for weeks after. And I had quite a mess to clean up.

So when you're reading one of those good books out there, be sure to take all appropriate safety precautions. Because one day at the library you may find a James Bond novel with greasy red spots in the middle and you'll know it's true—reading can be dangerous!

Biography:

Grew up: Elmira, New York, and Gainesville, Florida
Now lives: Elmira, New York
Random fact: Tall (6'5") but terrible at basketball

Selected Bibliography

Parts
More Parts
No Jumping on the Bed

DAVID BAUER

My Entire Football Career

People often ask me, "What's your favorite sport?" My answer is always the same: "Baseball."

But I grew up in Texas, and in Texas football was, and forever will be, king. I liked football a lot and played it all the time in my backyard and in my friends' backyards. And I played it pretty well. I was kind of small and was, let's say, not fast, but I could throw and catch a football as well as most of my buddies and better than a lot of them.

Just before sixth grade, my family moved to another house and a different school, and when I got there I found out that my new school had a six-man football team with uniforms and a schedule and everything. *Whoa*, I thought, *this is cool*, and they said I could join. The problem was that the team had already been practicing and, for reasons I couldn't fathom, they were all out of uniform jerseys. "You'll just have to get a jersey of your own," Coach said. The team's jerseys were a shiny deep green with white numbers, sort of like the Philadelphia Eagles'. Nowadays, you could easily go out and buy a green jersey with white numbers. Back then it wasn't easy at all. "Don't worry," said my mother. "I'll just get you a plain jersey and dye it green." *Okay, but what about the numbers, Mom?* "No, I can't make numbers," she said.

On the night before our first game, she presented me with my new jersey. A sick feeling filled my stomach. The jersey was the putrid color of canned English peas. Or stagnant pond water. It had no shine. And, as promised, no numbers. "Mom," I finally said, "I can't wear that." That was a mistake, of course.

"Well," she said, "I'm *so* sorry I couldn't make you a perfect uniform. I spent all day doing this for you and that's the thanks I get?" I was no match for her dual weapons of guilt and shame and quickly agreed that I was sure it would be fine.

As I trotted onto the field the next day to join my teammates in warm-up, I was consumed with new-guy dread. I knew how pathetic I looked. With my numberless pea-green jersey and oversized white helmet, I looked more like a cauliflower than a football player. I prayed that maybe these guys wouldn't pay any attention. "Your jersey looks like puke!" yelled my teammate Sam. And Sam was my new best friend. The rest of them just started laughing hysterically.

Six-man football, in the sixth grade, is really more like three-man football, at least on offense. You have a quarterback and a running back and an end. The other three are linemen, including the center. The big three do almost everything; the linemen do almost nothing. Our quarterback was Danny Armstrong, who was big and, I thought, very aptly named. Our running back was Teddy Vanderslice, who made terrible grades but could run faster than most horses. Sam was the end. I was the center.

Early in the game, as I was still getting used to the weird noises inside my helmet, I snapped the ball to Danny, who went back to pass. I took a couple of steps forward and turned to look back at Danny and see how the play was going. Not well. Both Sam and Teddy were covered and Danny was scrambling. Suddenly he looked right into my eyes and drilled a pass straight at me. I didn't even know I was an eligible receiver. Apparently I was.

I reacted brilliantly: as the ball came straight and hard into my gut, I wrapped my arms tightly around it. Two-yard gain! But with the surprise of the moment and the force of the throw (I'd like to say there was a vicious tackle, but I can't), I fell backward. I lay on the ground, still holding the ball tight to my stomach, and realized I could not breathe. For approximately forty-five minutes, or so it seemed, no air came into my body or went out of my body. Eventually, Coach came out to see why his pea-green center was still on his back on the ground. "What's the matter, kid?" he asked, with no trace of sympathy. I could say nothing. "You breathing?" Coach asked. I could see all my teammates encircling my body and staring down at me. They were silent but I could hear their thoughts: *Hey, the new kid's a weenie.* I could say nothing.

After what must have been several more hours without breath, Coach grabbed the waist of my pants and pulled me up in the air, lowered me, and pulled again. Life rushed back into my lungs. I had survived, but my teammates were less than impressed. "At least he didn't puke on his puke jersey!" said my best friend Sam. More hysterical laughter. The humiliation was total, and all for two yards.

I finished the game, and I finished the season, though I remember none of it. I had already decided that it was time for a career change.

And that's why I love baseball.

Biography:

Grew up: Dallas, Texas

Now lives: Larchmont, New York

Random fact: Learned the sport of snake crackin' in Texas. Get in a pickup truck, drive out into the country until you find a big snake sunning on a warm highway, grab him by the tail, whirl him around your head like a bullwhip, and snap his neck. This is probably illegal now.

Occupation: Deputy Managing Editor, *Sports Illustrated*

EDWARD BLOOR
Only a Game

Practically everywhere on Earth, people are ready to scream and fight and riot over the game that is known in the United States as soccer and everywhere else by variations of the word *football* (*el fútbol, de voetbal*, etc.). At least one war has been ignited by a soccer game—a World Cup qualifying match between El Salvador and Honduras in 1969. The "Soccer War" raged for over two weeks. Cities were bombed, and thousands died.

I grew up in a city that was populated in part by European immigrants, and they took soccer very seriously indeed. When I was eight years old, I began playing in a league that had teams with names like the Italian-Americans, the Polish-Americans, and the Ukrainian-Americans. I played for a mixed-ethnic team called Ideal Terminal (which, I believe, was the name of a trucking company). Back then, mixed-ethnic meant only that the players were not *all* Italian, or *all* Polish. They were, however, all white. In the case of Ideal Terminal, we were also all bad.

I remember playing against other eight-year-olds who, on the surface, looked just like me. But on the inside, these kids were steeled by a fearsome sense of purpose. They were backed up by screaming mobs of foreign-speaking parents, intent not only on winning soccer games but on settling ancient grudges begun in wars in Poland, Italy, or Ukraine. Ideal Terminal lost every game.

As fate would have it, I got to play on the same side as some of these soccer warriors when I got into high school. No thanks to me, we won the county and the state championships in my junior and senior years. We were fearsome, undefeated, and victorious because of a core of players for whom soccer was much more than a game.

I assumed that intensity would carry over into college, but it didn't. I discovered that my college did not have an actual soccer team. It did have a soccer "club." The players in the club might show up for practice, or they might not. They might show up for a game, or they might not. We lost our first game 11–0. We improved slightly in our second game, losing 10–1. Many players quit. For some reason, perhaps because I hadn't quit, I won the MVP trophy that year. This made me feel guilty about the thought of quitting myself, and it compelled me to play for a second year. But that was that. By the start of the third year, my soccer career was officially over. It was as dead as a Salvadoran referee in Honduras, or vice versa. Soccer just wasn't the same for me. It had become only a game.

Biography:

Grew up: Trenton, New Jersey

Now lives: Florida

Random fact: Used to teach, so he knows teachers need more respect

Selected Bibliography:

Tangerine
Story Time
Crusader

TONY DiTERLIZZI
Gondwanaland

In 1981, I stumbled upon a mysterious island out in the middle of the Pacific Ocean. It was inhabited by strange beings no man had ever seen before. There were weird lizardy-things that threw rocks at you, strange mucky-monsters who could swallow you whole, ice-breathing dragons, and an evil leader called Captain Bassolf, who captured any human foolish enough to stray into his castle and forced them into slavery.

I was only twelve years old when I arrived at this island, which I named Gondwanaland (after the prehistoric continent). I had been to places like this before—Middle Earth, Neverland, and Narnia to name a few—but they had been discovered by other adventurers. And they were bold adventurers, with bold names like J. R. R. Tolkien, C. S. Lewis, and Jules Verne. But as I said, this place was different—this place was discovered by me.

So, in between playing games of Dungeons and Dragons and watching *Star Wars*, I set out to make a record of all of the inhabitants that thrived on this island, in the form of a field guide. I began naming and describing all of the odd citizens of Gondwanaland. There were Tree-Dwellers, Suction-Cup Creatures, Swamp Wogs, and Seaweed Whirlyoids, and I drew pictures of every one of them. I hiked up every mountain, dove

CAPTIAN BASSOLF
(MEANIS TEARIS UPIS)

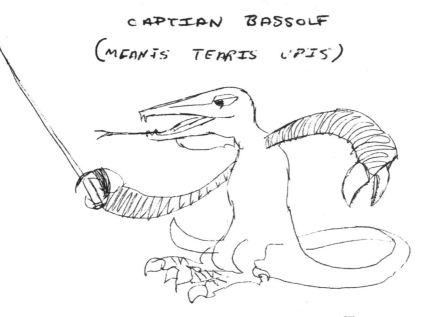

CAPTIAN BASSOLF IS RATHER SHORT (4FT) GREY WITH CYLINDER LIKE DEEP BLUE ARMS ENDING IN DIRTY YELLOW GRASPLIKE CLAWS. CAPTIAN BASSOLF IS A SLAVE MASTER WHO DIGS DOWN IN MINES FOR GOLD, SILVER DIAMONDS OR RUBIES. HE LIVES IN A RATHER SMALL CASTLE WITH LITTLE OR NO GUARDS, MOST OF THE WEAPONTRY WAS USED IN THE OLD WARS. LITTLE IS KNOWN ABOUT CAPTIAN BASSOLF FOR HE DOESNT GET ALONG WITH PEOPLE WELL. RUMOR HAS IT THAT THE CAPTIAN IS WITH OTHER VILLANS SELLING HIS PRICELESS GEMS FOR WEAPONTRY ALTHOUGH THIS HASNT BEEN VARIFIED, OTHERS SAY HE LETS YOU BOARD AT HIS CASTLE AND HE ATTACKS YOU & USES YOU FOR SLAVES. HIS loyal ASSISTANT SNIPER WILL BE DISCUSSED LATER. HE LIKES ANTIQUE WEAPONS TO COLLECT FROM HIS SOLD GEMS,

Here's my original story and sketch of Captain Bassolf. This was done in the classic medium of ballpoint pen and notebook paper.

in every lake, and drew detailed maps of the island (which, by the way, was shaped like a dinosaur skull).

Though Captain Bassolf was a meanie, he did know talent when he saw it, and he saw it in me. He told me to leave the island, go back home, and cultivate my love of drawing and telling stories.

I never returned to Gondwanaland. Every once in a while, I would open my guide to this magical place and long for it. Sure, I've been to other neat places and met other interesting characters, but nothing had quite the impact on me that this place did over twenty years ago.

So imagine my surprise when I was invited back. It seems Captain Bassolf had been keeping an eye on my career, and asked me to do a new portrait of him. Fortunately for me, he liked this one because it accurately portrayed his menacing demeanor.

Thanks, Captain, for inviting me back, and for seeing that my talents were much better suited for telling stories and not for mining gems.

Biography:

Grew up: Jupiter, Florida

Now lives: Amherst, Massachusetts

Random fact: Was obsessed with the Star Wars movies as a kid. Wanted to be Han Solo when he grew up.

Selected Bibliography:

Ted

The Spider and the Fly by Matt Hewitt

The Spiderwick Chronicles with Holly Black

Here's my new rendition of the captain.
In keeping with tradition, I also rendered
this image in ballpoint pen.

BRUCE BROOKS

E, A Minor, B7

There was only one thing you did in eighth grade, and I did it. I played in a band.

The irresistible imperative to grab three guys and start analyzing Ventures tunes swept through Takoma Park Junior High School as if the boys were random atoms suddenly bonded into identical molecules as a critical temperature was reached. It should be noted that we grabbed the other guys way before we grabbed actual musical instruments. We had some important decisions to make.

First, we had to decide who played what. This was pretty easy, seeing as no one in my band came cluttered with the restrictive precondition of actually playing a particular instrument. Also, there was only one assignment to decide—which of us would be designated to play drums. Everyone else would play guitar, talent later to be parsed into lead, rhythm, and bass (for which only the lowest two strings would be used; the bassist was the bottom of the food chain).

Picking the drummer was easy: the guy who played "Wipeout!" the best with his two forefingers would get the skins. It was close—we were all expert at digital "Wipeout!" of course— but I aced my colleagues. (And now it can be told: I cheated, supplying an extra essential short note in every phrase. Sorry.)

Next we had to name the band. After two weeks in which we did very little besides make six-second phone calls all night ("Hello?" "Hey, how about The Peroxides?" "Too long—it won't fit on the head of my bass drum." "Oh, right, yeah. Bye.") and pass one-word notes all day in school ("Antennas?" "Teamsters?" "Algebras?"), my colleagues and I settled on something. It was one of those bang-bang things: we were all sitting in the cafeteria, ignoring our Jell-O dessert ("Gelatins?"), when Charlie Dunba suddenly broke the silence of several seconds by smiling smugly and speaking the galvanic words, "The Bricks."

The rest is history. From September to June, we did nothing but be Bricks. This involved, first, going as a foursome to one of the seven music stores in town every Saturday morning, making the clerks (all very snarky high school musicians) hand us down electric guitar after electric guitar, playing the sequence of E, A minor, B7 in the 4-4-2-2-4 pattern. Next we shuffled to one of three record stores (as a foursome, *toujours*) where we made the clerks (eye-rolling high school electronics freaks) play us song after song (on 45s), to which we listened by squinching our ears together around a single plastic earphone. When, after long debate and many re-listens, we had decided on five or six new tunes to add to our repertoire, we went to the Little Tavern or Hot Shoppe to talk in loud voices about these things alongside The Magentas and The Skids and The Cluster and (perhaps the coolest band) The Woefuls.

Every school day, as soon as the last bell rang, we lingered in the hall at our lockers and shouted over the hurrying throng, "Hey, what time's *practice* tonight?" or "We *practicing* over at VeeKay's tonight?" If you couldn't demonstrate that you had a band practice to go to at night, you simply were not a serious guy.

And, indeed, we practiced. One of the guys got a guitar for his birthday—a Silvertone, from Sears. I bought a pair of Ludwig drumsticks, and, hey, we were set to boogie. Our bass player's father drove an ice-cream truck, and he let his kid bring two of the heavy cardboard twenty-gallon containers (empty, alas) to the basement where we toiled, and suddenly I was the loudest musician in the band. Our rhythm and bass never managed to get guitars, and our lead never got an amplifier—I didn't really need drums—but we never stopped listening and analyzing and rehearsing until spring. To this day I know the simpler chords, the melody lines, and the tom-toms fills to almost every radio hit from 1963–64. The same is true, I'm sure, for all my two hundred coequals from The Viscounts and The Tropicals and The Cakes.

Of the nearly fifty bands that comprised the entire boy population of the Takoma Park eighth grade that year, only one managed to acquire four instruments and at least one amp. They also managed to rent a half hour in a Wheaton studio and record "Mrs. Brown You've Got a Lovely Daughter" (instrumental version) and "Pipeline," which the lead player's rich father paid to have pressed into twenty-five 45-rpm records. We of the other bands decided they had sold out. We were right: at the start of school the next September, these guys were still together, still having practices, yearning to trade up their axes, analyzing surfing songs. But now they were losers. Bands were eighth grade. *Nobody* played in a band in ninth grade. Ninth grade, it turned out, was about girls.

Biography:

Grew up: Washington, D.C., and rural North Carolina

Now lives: Brooklyn, New York

Random fact: Has repeatedly been asked, "Why do you look like a mad scientist?"

Selected Bibliography:

Midnight Hour Encores
The Moves Make the Man
What Hearts

WILLIAM G. BROZO

My Brilliant Invention

A couple of months ago, a smart-aleck friend of mine sent me a bumper sticker that read, I SURVIVED CATHOLIC SCHOOL. I immediately got on the phone to tell him, *No I didn't!* Like many of my peers who spent their grammar school years in traditional Catholic schools, I have some fond memories—but also bitter ones.

One of the truly fond memories I have of St. Philip's is of my third-grade teacher, Sister Bernadette. Petite, attractive (as nuns go), and generally friendly, she turned me on to books like no other. It was due to her encouragement that I discovered biography, which I've enjoyed unstintingly since then. From her well-stocked classroom bookcase, I read about Robert Fulton, the great steamboat inventor; Samuel F. B. Morse, the perfector of the telegraph; Thomas Edison, inventor of nearly everything else; and then there was Alexander Graham Bell.

The story of Bell's life and his work on the telephone was enthralling for this budding tinkerer. After reading about these great inventors, I would race to the garage, burning with inspiration to invent something myself. Mostly, however, I created a mess of my father's workbench, got punished for leaving tools out, and was left pondering what to do with a useless mélange of gears, rubber bands, springs, batteries, and wire. The Bell biography was different, though. The author told of his early experimentation with tin cans—which when connected by a taut string, could convey one's voice. Finally, an invention I could reproduce.

Ignoring my older brother's warnings, I placed my cans, stripped of their cream corn labels and joined by twine, in my book satchel. During recess, my friend and neighbor, Larry Trevino, and I managed to rig the crude communication system in such a way that neither of us could be seen by the other, though we could hear each other's voices perfectly well. Before long, we fell into what had just become our favorite pastime, trading libels about our Mother Principal, known privately as "tons o' fun"—when suddenly her deep, urgent voice rattled in the tin can in my ear: "Mr. Brozo, come to my office this instant and bring this contraption with you!" As fate would have it, on her random patrols of the school's small campus, she had come upon Larry with the metal cylinder to his ear. Curious, she drew nearer until he caught a glimpse of her and took off running. She picked up the crude handset in time to catch my last scurrilities. I walked down the hall quaking with fear and fantasizing about the possible instruments of torture at Mother Superior's disposal.

A verbal brow beating left me in tears, but seemed too easy given the seriousness of my iniquity. "Now get back to your classroom and I'll have something more for you there."

No sooner had I returned to Sister Bernadette's room, when Mother Superior's voice crackled in the intercom speaker. "Sister Bernadette, I want two of your students, William Brozo and Lawrence Trevino, to demonstrate for the rest of your pupils their homemade walkie-talkie set. And I want them to say what I overheard them say during recess. I'll listen in."

Well, the rest is history. Public humiliation was a favorite form of punishment at my school. The spanking I got later from my father only added insult to injury. But I didn't give up on the tin-can phones just yet. Larry, who lived across the street, agreed to string them between his attic bedroom window and mine. We maintained secret contact well past bedtime for an entire summer. Nonetheless, even to this day, when I see a kid in the mall chattering on a cell phone, the specter of Mother Superior flits in and out of my consciousness.

Biography:

Grew up: Detroit, Michigan

Now lives: Vienna, Virginia (just outside of Washington, D.C.)

Random fact: Is a literacy volunteer for secondary teachers in a USAID project in Macedonia

Selected Bibliography:

To Be a Boy, to Be a Reader: Engaging Teen and Preteen Boys in Active Literacy

Readers, Teachers, Learners: Expanding Literacy across the Content Areas with Michele L. Simpson

MICHAEL CART
A Real Guy

My dad was a real guy. He'd been a football hero in high school, my dad, and, as an adult, he worked with his hands and listened to sports on the radio in his shop—the garage behind our house— where he cleaned car radiators and built iron scaffolding, which he then rented out to make money to feed his family (that'd be my mom, my twin sister, and me). He spent a lot of time in his shop, my dad, and every once in a while, usually when he'd had one beer too many and was feeling expansive, he'd call me out there to "help" him. My blood would run cold when I heard his slurred summons, and I'd start to sweat. Because I knew *I* wasn't a real guy. I was fat and clumsy, I loved to read, and I made straight As in school. And my dad scared the living daylights out of me because—with his red face, short fuse, and explosive temper—he was like a five foot eight inch–tall firecracker waiting to explode.

"Hand me that socket wrench," he'd snap. His shop, made of concrete blocks with hard edges, was not a friendly place to soft people like me. And so I, not having a clue what a socket wrench was, would shut my eyes and grab the nearest tool, praying it was what he wanted. It never was, of course, and after about five minutes of suffering my ineptness, he'd explode, my firecracker guy, and snarl, "Go inside and help your mother." It was the worst thing he could imagine saying to a boy.

But I figured it was my due. And so, off I scurried. And you know what? I may not have been much help to my dad, but I got to be pretty good at helping my mom—by vacuuming rugs, changing beds, and dusting furniture.

I was also good at something else—I was good at school. I loved books, you see, and I dreamed of becoming a writer. But because I was lousy at sports—and because I was a fat, straight-A teacher's pet, to boot—I became the subject of a lot of teasing from the real guys. One of the guys in particular—let's call him "Eddie"—liked to back me into dark corners and shove his lean, handsome, muscular face into mine and call me names. He had a dimple in his right cheek when he smiled, but I never saw it on those dead-serious occasions.

Eddie was a real guy, a natural athlete who grew up to be a star of our high school basketball team. I lived in Indiana then, so this was a really big deal.

I *was* fat. But worse, I was also afraid. So I didn't dare challenge Eddie. Instead, I simply stood there, silent as a cantaloupe, backed up against a handy tree by my tormentor. Until he got tired, that is, and let me escape, to run home and cry to my mother. Who ultimately betrayed me by telling my father about my tormentor.

His response was to drink a six-pack of beer and decide that this time my plight was personal. Somehow, his son's failure to be a real guy invalidated his own guyness.

So that's how it happened that I found myself perched precariously on the handlebars of my bicycle while my father, three sheets to the wind and all red in the face, pedaled us both to Eddie's house, where—Dad dictated—I would stand up to my tormentor. And if I couldn't, well, then he personally would whip the ass of Eddie's old man.

I still see the picture in my mind's eye: a pale, blond, frightened fat boy and a drunk, angry, red-faced firecracker of a man, two unlikely comrades on a bicycle built for one, both headed for vengeance . . . or humiliation.

But real life isn't as conclusive as fiction. We finally arrived at Eddie's house, all right, but only to find that neither he nor his father was at home. I was relieved, the crisis averted; my dad was disappointed. Together, in silence, we returned home.

The next morning I went on a diet. Nobody told me I had to. It was my decision. I lost twenty-five pounds in a month.

For the first time in my life I looked like a real guy.

But inside, where it mattered, I remained the same fat, book-loving boy who didn't know the difference between a socket wrench and a piece of elbow macaroni.

I still don't.

And I still take an automatic, though now metaphorical, step back from the lives of the "real" guys who continue to surround me and, quietly, I observe what the Eddies of today are up to.

And then I turn my observations into words and put them down on paper. That's how I finally grew up to become a writer and, come to think of it, a darned lucky guy!

Biography:
Grew up: Logansport, Indiana
Now lives: San Diego, California
Random fact: Has a collection of over 9,000 books

Selected Bibliography:
Necessary Noise: Stories about Our Families as They Really Are (ed.)

Tomorrowland: Ten Stories about the Future (ed.)

Rush Hour Volume Two: Bad Boys: A Journal of Contemporary Voices (ed.)

PETER CHERCHES
My Life of Crime

When I was ten years old I was involved in organized crime. Not the Mafia. Nothing like that. We didn't kill anyone or break any legs. It was a shoplifting ring.

It was a local operation, in my neighborhood in Brooklyn, New York. I lived in a solidly middle-class neighborhood—not a high-crime neighborhood at all. The residents were mostly Jewish and Catholic (Irish and Italian), but back then, in the mid-sixties, the Jews and the Catholics in my neighborhood didn't mix too much, so I hung out with a mostly Jewish crowd.

Many of us had already been shoplifting from the local candy stores and supermarkets, and at one point a bunch of us decided to band together and combine forces, figuring there was strength and efficiency in numbers. Some of the kids felt we needed a ringleader, but others, myself included, felt that it should be one for all and all for one. The majority were in the ringleader camp, but when it came time for a vote, nobody could agree on a leader. So it was decided that a ringleader would be recruited from outside the group, and that the candidate must have particularly strong credentials.

To many of the kids, that meant only one person—the notorious Butch Goldstein, Jewish thug. Butch was fourteen and his résumé was impressive: he had beaten up numerous kids, talked back to grown-ups for years, killed the pets of several of his enemies, and stolen more than the rest of us put together. I neither liked nor trusted Butch and I felt that to make him ringleader would be a dangerous move, but apparently most of the others believed there was indeed honor among thieves.

Well, Butch certainly got us organized. No longer would there be haphazard shoplifting; now we'd have teams and shifts. Butch called the shots. He told us what to steal and how much of it. He gave us pointers on technique. Two or three kids would go into Janoff's candy store, or Fred and Rudy's, and while one kid acted as a decoy, ordering a malted or an egg cream to occupy the attention of the man behind the counter, the others would carefully slide packs of gum and boxes of Jujubes and Dots and Junior Mints into their pockets. We had several large cartons to store the candy in, hidden in the basement of the apartment building I lived in. The idea, so Butch told us, was that we'd collect the stuff for a month or two, and then it would be doled out equally. That way, he said, it would be really special when we finally split up the booty— we could have a big party. It sounded like a good idea, but several days before the candy was to be divvied up, a couple of the kids went to the basement to deposit their take for the day and discovered that the cartons were missing. They called a meeting, rank and file, without Butch. We all agreed that Butch and only Butch could be responsible for such a dastardly deed, but when we confronted him, he played dumb. He said the candy must have been stolen by some Catholic kids who had gotten wind of our shoplifting ring.

This betrayal cured most of us of our criminal inclinations, and the shoplifting ring broke up. I think most of us have gone on to lead pretty honest, law-abiding lives.

As for Butch, the last I heard he was arrested somewhere in Texas for passing bad checks. I must confess that I have changed his name here because I'm still afraid of him, nearly forty years later.

Biography:

Grew up: Brooklyn, New York, and grew up even more in Manhattan
Now lives: Brooklyn, New York (stopped growing up)
Random fact: Played kazoo for money

Selected Bibliography:

Condensed Book
Between a Dream and a Cup of Coffee

TIMOTHY BASIL ERING
Triplets

Years ago, I packed a small collection of my childhood art into a cardboard box.

That box is scarred now from repeated mouse attacks, and limp from being in a Cape Cod basement that floods when it rains at high tide. But still protected in it are precious mementoes, including my fifth-grade book of poems.

"I did this!" I reminded myself, as I looked through the pages, which include my attempts to illustrate the nine different forms of poetry we learned.

Boy, I remember how proud I was. How many times did I wander by the display table at the school fair, to peek again at the honorable mention ribbon on this book! Looking at these old poems and illustrations, I am reminded that everything big or small must start somewhere.

After the school fair, I remember feeling for the first time this secret magical emotion, like a giant hand was patting me on the back, rewarding me for creating something. No one could see the giant hand, nor could they see that I was dripping with diamonds and gold as I scurried home, leaping over a dozen puddles at a time.

FRIPLETS

I saw a little mouse.
Knittin' a little blouse.
In her little house.

Witches are so mean.
Their faces are obscene.
Watch-out on Halloween!

3.

I'm still proud of these old poems and the detail in my old drawings (that tiny mouse house door, and those warts on that witch's nose), but boy, could they use a little salt and pepper! So I thought if I made new drawings, I could bring out a little whimsy.

I don't use colored Magic Marker much anymore, so for the new drawings I used ink and some paint. Also, I felt that after all these years, we should finally find out who that tiny mouse is. And, of course, that witch was begging for a broom and some attitude!

I saw a little mouse.
Knittin' a little blouse,
In her little house.

Biography:
Grew up: Cape Cod, Massachusetts
Now lives: Somerville, Massachusetts
Random fact: Has webbed toes, second and middle toe, both feet

Witches are so mean.
Their faces are obscene.
Watch out on Halloween!

Selected Bibliography:

The Story of Frog Belly Rat Bone
The Tale of Despereaux by Kate DiCamillo

EOIN COLFER
The Legend of Tripod

I remember seeing the World Book Day books come flooding into my classroom one year. Everyone had them. Free books—of course they had. And what's more, they were actually reading them. Several were hooked by the experience.

That'll do for me, I thought. *When I get famous, I will not turn down the offer to do a World Book Day book.* How noble of me. At the time, I had written approximately enough to cover two sides of a postcard. Double-spaced.

Years passed and still the WBD people did not contact my people. I never gave up hope. *Someday they will come to me*, I thought. *They will come and beg me to save children's literature, and possibly education.* This thought kept me going through rejection slips, discarded flowchart book plans, and six years in a bamboo cage on Mount Fuji. Okay, some of this paragraph is not true, but I have already sold the rights to Miramax, so it stays in the story.

Finally, the big day arrived: the World Book Day people called my publishers. By this time I had made a name for myself writing stories about a nasty teenager named Artemis Fowl and his farting dwarf sidekick. But no more thrills and spills rock'em-sock'em projects for me. I was a World Book Day author now. Time for some class.

After several months of research, the bones of a story began to form in my mind. Something sensitive enough to appeal to the modern young adult. Something with a solid moral message to inspire the readers, yet in no way patronizing.

My hero was a horse who loses a leg in a polo pileup. This horse, nicknamed "Tripod" by his cruel owners, vows to win the Grand National in spite of his leg shortage problem. After years of training alone, at night, possibly in the rain, Tripod triumphs. As he crosses the finish line, he spots his long-lost mother in the crowd. Beautiful. I still get chills.

A meeting was scheduled with the WBD people so I could pitch *The Legend of Tripod*. We met in the Burger King on Leicester Square. All expense spared. I slid my book plan across the table to the WBD representatives. There were two of them. A man and a woman. Mean-looking individuals in black suits.

They flipped the plan open and began to read. Nothing was said for several moments. Finally, they spoke.

"It's not that we don't like it," said the woman.

"Yeah, we like it, don't get us wrong."

"That bit about the steeplechase, that was hilarious."

Hilarious? Not the word I was hoping for.

"Hilarious. Really. Three legs—that cracked me up."

"But the thing is . . ."

"We want the little man."

"Yeah, the dwarf. You know, the one with the problem."

I played stupid. "What problem?"

"The farting, Colfer! The farting, OK? We want the farting dwarf."

"But I'm finished with all that now," I objected. "I'm a serious writer. What about Tripod? Did you read the bit about his mother? It's literature. The children deserve it."

They both leaned across the table.

"We thought the dwarf could steal something. He's a thief, right?"

"I s'pose," I mumbled.

"He could team up with the obnoxious kid, Arthur Chicken."

"Artemis Fowl," I corrected.

"Whatever. Well maybe they could team up and steal something. Now you can go with the pony story if you feel that's the right thing to do. But I can guarantee you that Tripod will never see the light of day."

I stuffed Tripod into my jacket. These people were playing hardball.

"I need to think about it. I can't plan a book just like that."

The man patted a bulge under his arm. "Think about it, Colfer. But don't take too long. World Book Day is coming up soon and we need time to slash—sorry, edit—the masterpiece that I feel sure you will be giving us."

I left, feeling shaken to my core, and took a cab to Luton.

Nevertheless, I decided that it might be prudent to submit an Artemis Fowl story for World Book Day. Something original, though, not the rubbish the WBD people had suggested. So I toiled for a month and finally came up with a plotline I was happy with. In this episode, Artemis teams up with Mulch Diggums, a flatulent dwarf, to steal a diamond tiara, with hilarious consequences.

Before e-mailing the story in, I added a defiant line: "Tripod will return."

Biography:

Grew up: Wexford, Ireland

Now lives: Wexford, Ireland

Random fact: Originally wanted to be a comic book artist, and still spends a lot of time and money on comics even though he is a mature adult, according to him

Selected Bibliography:

Artemis Fowl • *Artemis Fowl: The Arctic Incident* • *The Legend of Spud Murphy* illustrated by Glenn McCoy

CHRIS CRUTCHER
"O" *Foods*

Any teenage male who could fog up a mirror placed under his nose in Cascade, Idaho, in the early sixties played high school sports. If football practice started in the late summer of your freshman year and you didn't show up, they came and got you. And your parents let them in. Your choice was to get beat up in pads or out of pads. I was, in 1960, a 123-pound offensive guard, with grass stains on my back and cleat marks on my chest to prove it.

If you hung in there a few years, even with my limited ability, you'd finally play; that was the good news and the bad, because if you played you lettered and if you lettered you joined the "C" Club. And if you joined the "C" Club, your relationship with one food group changed forever. The "O" foods. Oysters and olives.

When I stand onstage in a high school auditorium these days, I try to convince the students before me that we are alike, that I have earned the right to tell stories about people their age from having lived through that age myself, and that the seventeen-year-old Chris Crutcher of 1964 is more like the contemporary seventeen-year-old than he is different. Which is why I *never* tell them about Cascade High School's "C" Club initiation.

And here I break my code of silence.

"C" Club president Ron Hall gathers the new lettermen in a classroom after school on initiation day and instructs us to be at the gym at 7:00 that evening. Sharp. "Shower good," he says. "Get your mind right."

Showered good, our minds right, the gymnasium doors slam shut on us at 7:00 sharp. Each of us turns over to a veteran letterman a twenty-seven-inch, ten-holed, beveled-edged hardwood paddle we made in shop class, an action I consider akin to buying the rope and crafting the noose, then handing it over to your hangman.

Stripped to our pasty white birthday suits, we're led to a table lined with small mason jars filled with slimy gray oysters. We are *so* lucky, we learn. Oysters such as these are an expensive delicacy; many Cascade graduates will be ten years out of college before they earn enough to ingest food such as this.

We are to swallow them raw.

I close my eyes, imagine Jell-O. But at best, it's fishy Jell-O, every bit as likely as the oysters themselves to trigger my gag reflex. Not to worry. My gag reflex plays an integral part in this exercise. These are *expensive* oysters, they tell us again—not bought and paid for, but, rather, rented. They need them back. Strings are tied to our oysters.

Any student of biology will tell you all humans have muscles—voluntary and involuntary—that hum along doing their jobs far below our conscious radar—allowing us to breathe, or say, pass on food without thinking—*until*, as anyone who has undergone any procedure ending in "-oscopy" will tell you, those muscles are engaged in some manner unintended by nature—like *backward*! Raw oysters on the way down may be unsavory; raw oysters on a yo-yo string tickle the edges of the imagination.

But you could not see to where we go next with the Hubble telescope, even from the very farthest edge of your imagination: the olive race.

Seven naked letterboys crouch on hands and knees next to seven naked letterboys' shoes, staring down the basketball court at seven black unpitted olives. At the sound of the cap pistol, we are to race-crawl the length of the gym, sit on the olives to pick them up, and race back down court to drop them in our shoes. The loser gets to eat one of the olives, picked at random. This is truly the stuff of which real men are made.

Thanks to my grandfather and my mother, I am the odds-on favorite to be bringing up the rear, as it were, on this one. Neither of them has a butt, and that particular DNA coursed directly down my family's genetic river to me. Crudely put, our butts are the vortex of our legs. There is none of the cushy flab necessary to cradle an olive for a ninety-foot run.

I have choked a number of times in spectacular fashion in my short high school career, from missing a tackle that would certainly have preserved our lead in a regional championship game to dropping the baton in an 880 relay exchange, but if I choke now, I choke twice—once in the race and once on the olive— and as I squat on my third desperate attempt to gain purchase on my olive I am running dead last. Leonard Irwin, running next to last, crosses the half-court line as I finally get it to stick and rise to waddle back to my shoe. He lowers his dark nugget toward his shoe as I cross the free-throw line, looking up with a smirk that says, *Better you than me, Crutcher, you poor buttless bastard.*

Only there *is* a God and he is a wrathful God and Leonard Irwin must have done something way worse in his young life than I have in mine, because *he misses his shoe.*

My father was a World War II B-17 bomber pilot, known for demanding exquisite precision of his bombardier, and some of *that* DNA must also have flowed to me down that same generational river, because I hear that black nugget hit the inside heel of my Chuck Taylor Converse All-Star tennis shoe and roll to the toe and I know it is Leonard Irwin and not I who has just bought a one-way ticket to Gag City.

I could describe the remainder of the evening's events and

put this book high on the banned book list for the year, but suffice it to say that we played two variations of a game called Choo-Choo, and engaged in an exercise that included a string, a bucket of bolts, and an appendage that was not an arm or a leg. We wrapped up our evening substituting Tabasco sauce for Preparation H.

President Hall ushered us to the bleachers when we'd showered and dressed, praising us for following so many brilliant Cascade Ramblers who had gone before through our rite of passage toward manhood. "We are a select and courageous group," he said. "And we shall be stoic, sworn to silence. He who demonstrates such weakness as to divulge the events that went on here this evening shall suffer the curse of all ancestral Ramblers."

That was back in the spring of 1963. I believe I am the first to squeal.

Biography:

Grew up: Cascade, Idaho

Now lives: Spokane, Washington

Random fact: Lost his teeth to a girl with a Louisville Slugger at age fourteen, then turned misfortune into gold when he placed his plastic clackers in a hamburger bun and performed a ventriloquist act with "Hamilton Burger, the Burger That Bites Back," winning third place in his high school talent show

Selected Bibliography:

Ironman

Whale Talk

King of the Mild Frontier: An Ill-Advised Autobiography

TERRY DAVIS
What I'm Telling You Is the Truth

I wish my dad had liked me. If we'd been friends I'd be a different man.

Reader, I know what you're thinking: *Oh, boo, hoo, hoo, Davis! Boo hoo! Don't you baby boomer wussies ever stop whining?*

Weak as it is, guys, what I'm telling you is the truth.

My father didn't like me. He just flat-out didn't enjoy having me around. This was the gravity force of my boyhood, and as gravity does, it pulled me into a smaller, denser thing. If my mother and her folks hadn't liked me *so* much, that gravity would have pulled me inside out.

Davis, you're thinking, *how can a father not like his son? Fathers love their sons. That's biology. That's how life works.*

Maybe it is. My dad said he loved me. And he gave me all kinds of stuff, including money, when I needed it, which was often.

Dad's name was Roy. Roy Davis, no middle name or initial. He was in the car business all his working life. When I was in graduate school at the University of Iowa in '71 and my old VW went to hell, he bought me a car, drove it to Iowa City, and caught a plane back to Spokane. When I was living in Rio de Janeiro in '73, he sent me a little transistor radio with an ear plug so I could listen all the time and learn Portuguese. When my entire life went down the toilet in '80, he gave me one of his rental houses so I'd have a place to live. It breaks my heart when I think back on these gestures of affection he made to me.

The thing is this: I'd give a zillion times every nickel he ever gave me if I could live my boyhood over as his friend.

What's it mean for a father to be a friend to his son? It means he can't keep the smile off his face when his boy walks into the room—like I can't keep the smile off my face when Pascal or Joshie or Sasha breaks over the horizon, because they're just too much fun to have around.

I wish my dad had let me know him. I needed to know what a man was. He could have told me this by telling me who he was, but he didn't. I must have asked him in my head a hundred times if you were still afraid of the dark when you got to be a man.

I loved sports for the pure joy of playing. But I played so hard in organized sports to earn the respect and affection of my coaches. Nothing made me feel better when I was a boy than to swing my bike up to the baseball diamond and see in Coach Cobb's face that he was glad Davis had shown up. Years later when I became a teacher and a coach, I tried to put that look on my face for every kid. For some kids the look was a lie, but I held it there as long as I could.

When *Vision Quest*, my first novel, became a movie, Dad barked at me to do something smart with the money. He didn't say he was proud of me, but I could tell he was. Being a writer—or an *artist*—to him was being a misdirected soul. What a man did was work eight to five—or eight to eight when you were on till closing—and pick up a check every two weeks. But somehow I had hit the winning number with that little book. *If Rock and Roll Were a Machine*, my third novel, is about the kid I really was; *Vision Quest* is about the kid I wished I was and maybe could have been.

My father was so tough that something in me didn't believe he would ever die. Emphysema did a job on him, though. Still, no matter how sick he was, when we talked on the phone, his voice always carried that commanding resonance.

I was worried when Mom called and told me he was in the hospital again and that I'd better get on a plane. I spent two nights at home with Mom, who had emphysema, too. She was the one who looked like she was dying, but Dad was the one hospitalized.

He didn't look great, but he sure didn't look as sick as his wife of fifty years. If I closed my eyes when he was talking, I heard that eternal voice again. He might as well have been at his desk with a cigar in his mouth, or his pipe, closing a deal on another Olds Cutlass.

The TV cut from pro football to a Mr. Goodwrench commercial. I looked up at the actor in his General Motors blue and white striped shirt. "That's what I should have been," I said. "I should have been a mechanic."

"You should have been a writer," Dad barked.

I looked at him there, propped up in the hospital bed with the metal rails. He was wearing his blue and white striped robe from home. We had the same wild tuft of white chest hair sticking out the necks of our T-shirts. Something in me recognized the possibility that my father was *affirming* me, telling me that I had taken the right path in life even though it was a path he couldn't see no matter how hard or how long he looked. But he said it in the same tone he'd used with me for fifty years, and so I couldn't take that possibility to heart.

I didn't say anything then. I told him good-bye, that I loved him, that I'd see him again. But there was a phone message waiting for me at the Northwest counter. Mom had called to say Dad died.

My father had probably been trying to make his peace with me. I'm sure he had, in fact. Believe me, I wanted to hear it. But it was too late. I'd gone deaf to the possibility.

Biography:

Grew up: Spokane, Washington
Now lives: Minnesota
Random fact: Was a wrestler, then a wrestling coach

Selected Bibliography:

Vision Quest
Mysterious Ways
If Rock & Roll Were a Machine

ESQUIRE
The Rules

There is a legend that a leather-bound, handwritten book with the simple title *The Rules* was once discovered in the research library of *Esquire* magazine. The story goes that now, every third Tuesday of every month, an *Esquire* staff member consults the book and jots down whichever rules catch his eye. These are then published in *Esquire* in an effort to provide "just a fraction of the plenitude of wisdom contained in the rules."

Rule 21.
Talk half as much as you listen.

Rule 91.
Never play cards with a man who wears a visor.

Rule 95.
Right fielders are the ugliest.

Rule 119.
Never trust anyone who uses unusual paper clips.

Rule 237.
It's always unacceptable to refuse a woman's request to dance.

Rule 324.

You know you've made it when there's a bobblehead doll of you.

Rule 341.

Do not give yourself a nickname.

Rule 359.

Women who have two or more brothers are less likely to be disgusted by you.

Rule 364.

Bald umpires are excellent, no matter the sport.

Rule 372.

When in doubt, pick "C."

Rule 374.

Minor league ballparks serve the best hot dogs.

Rule 468.

Never order a Sloppy Joe on a first date.

Rule 470.

If your dream involves an elaborate plot in which you are looking for a bathroom, it's time to get up and take a pee.

Rule 498.

Oddly, both of the following statements are true: Monkeys are never funnier than when they are wearing clothing. And: Monkeys are never sadder than when they're wearing clothing.

MATT GROENING

LIFE IN HELL

Any Questions, Class?

© 1987 BY MATT GROENING

Biography:

Grew up: Portland, Oregon

Now lives: Happy that he can pay his rent

Random fact: Parents named Homer and Marge. Sisters named Lisa and Maggie.

Selected Bibliography:

School Is Hell • *Childhood Is Hell* • *Simpsons Comics Extravaganza*

DOUGLAS FLORIAN
Guide for Guys

Don't slouch
Don't slurp
Don't belch
Don't burp

Don't snort
Don't snore
Don't be
A bore

Don't daze
Don't doze
Don't pick
Your nose

Don't taunt
Don't tease
Don't lose
Your keys

Don't pinch
Don't poke
Don't smack
Don't smoke

Don't laze
Don't loaf
Don't be
An oaf

Don't sneak
Don't snivel
Don't double dribble

Don't punch
Don't box
Don't wear
Smelly socks

Don't lurch
Don't limp
Don't be
A wimp

Don't whine
Don't cry
Just be
A good guy

Biography:

Grew up: New York City
Now lives: New York City
Random fact: Collected stamps and built model planes
as a kid

Selected Bibliography:

Mammalabilia
Insectlopedia
In the Swim

NEIL GAIMAN

Why Books Are Dangerous

When I was a boy, I was almost always carrying a book. It might not have been obvious. Paperbacks were fairly easy to slip into pockets, after all. My father would frisk me for books before family weddings or funerals; otherwise he knew that, while other people were being bored, I'd be sitting comfortably, probably under a table, off in my own world, reading.

I liked books. I did not yet suspect that books were dangerous. I didn't care what the books were about, as long as they had a story of some kind—spy stories, horror stories, SF or fantasy, histories, adventures, tales. I'd read true-life stories about people who caught spies or captured rare animals for zoos or people who hunted down man-eating tigers. I also was very fond of detectives and the books they came in. These were, I think, looking back on it, all very sensible things for a boy to like, and not the least bit dangerous.

The headmaster of my school in the south of England, a pipe-smoking, gruff gentleman who was famous for his precise and painful use of the slipper on boys who were sent to him for misbehaving, once confiscated a book from me. It was called *And to my nephew Albert I leave the island what I won off Fatty Hagen in a poker game*, and it had a photograph of a naked lady on the cover, which was why it was confiscated. This seemed particularly unfair, as in the early 1970s, most books seemed to have naked ladies on the covers, which, at least in the case of *And to my nephew Albert . . .* political comedy, had little or nothing to do with what was going on inside the book. I was interrogated by the headmaster and was given the book back at the end of term, with a warning to watch what I read. He didn't use the slipper, though. Not that time.

Obviously the headmaster understood the dangers of books. He was trying to tell me something. I didn't listen.

Eventually I started to read the dangerous books.

The really dangerous books had titles like *1001 Jolly Interesting Things a Boy Can Do.* You could make dyes from common garden vegetables. It explained it all.

I read the article on making dyes from common garden vegetables, and then I boiled a beetroot and soaked a white school shirt in the beet water, and turned it a purply sort of red. I decided that I wouldn't be caught dead wearing it. Then I put it in the washing, and it turned all the shirts and socks and underwear it was washed with a rather startling shade of pink.

I had not learned my lesson. The next thing I found was the toffee recipe.

I learned that if I melted some butter in a saucepan, and then added sugar and golden syrup and a tablespoon of water, and I heated it all together and got it very hot (but didn't burn it), and dripped drops of the boiling liquid into a glass of cold water, when the drops went solid, it was done. Then I'd pour it out onto a greased pie-pan, and let it set hard.

I was so proud. I'd made a golden-clear, buttery toffee. Pure sugar, with a little fat. It tasted amazing. Chewing it was a battle between the toffee and my teeth. Sometimes my teeth would win, sometimes the toffee would prove the victor and pull out a filling, or deal with a loose tooth.

This went on for several months.

I was, I think, in a math lesson. I'd put a fist-sized lump of the toffee into my pocket, where it had melted, slowly, to the shape of my leg. And I had forgotten about it. I also had a handkerchief in the pocket.

"You. Boy," said the teacher. "Gaiman. You're snivelling, boy. Blow your nose."

I said, "Yes, sir," and pulled the handkerchief from the pocket. It came out, and as it did so, a large lump of toffee that was stuck to the handkerchief sailed out across the room and hit the tiled floor.

It shattered when it hit the floor, like glass, into several hundred sharp-edged fragments.

I spent the rest of the lesson on my knees, picking up the sticky-sharp bits of toffee from the floor, while the teacher, convinced that I had done this on purpose to be funny (as if I'd waste a huge lump of toffee on a joke), made sarcastic comments. And, at the end of the lesson, I was sent to the headmaster with a note explaining what I'd done.

The headmaster read the note, puffed on his pipe, then walked slowly to the cupboard at the back of his study and, opening it, produced a large tartan slipper, and suggested that I might want to bend over.

That was the day I discovered that books were dangerous.

At least, books that suggested you do something. . . .

Biography:

Grew up: England

Now lives: America

Random fact: Is a member of the Weird Bunny of the Month Club, and every month receives a really disturbing stuffed rabbit

Selected Bibliography:

Good Omens with Terry Pratchett
The Wolves in the Walls illustrated by Dave McKean
The Sandman

BRETT HELQUIST

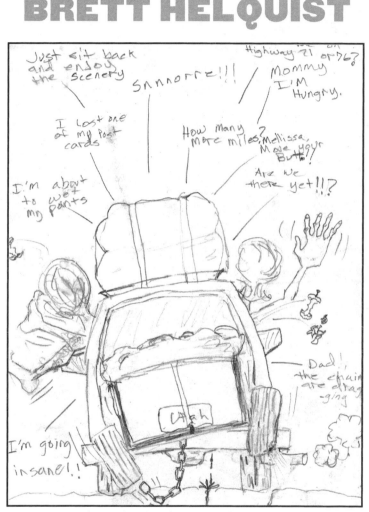

Young Brett draws his family's typical summer vacation trip.

I grew up in a large family. Every summer, Mom and Dad loaded
us into the car for summer vacation. We had a lot of fun, but with
seven kids in a cramped space and long hours on the road, there
was a lot of insanity, too. Years later when I drew the picture on
the next page of the Baudelaire kids in the trunk of Count Olaf's
car (trust me, you can't see them but they're in there) I knew just
how they felt.

©2002 Brett Helquist

Biography:

Grew up: Orem, Utah

Now lives: Brooklyn, New York

Random fact: Favorite thing to do when not drawing pictures is playing guitar and banjo—old blues and ragtime

Selected Bibliography:

A Series of Unfortunate Events books by Lemony Snicket • *Chasing Vermeer* by Blue Balliett • *Roger, the Jolly Pirate*

JACK GANTOS

The Follower

My mother said he was trouble the first time I met him. His name was Frankie Pagoda and he had just been catapulted across his yard like a human cannonball and landed badly in ours. He was moaning as I stood over him, not knowing what to do. He was on his back and at first he wasn't moving, but slowly he began to gyrate his arms and legs like a stunned crab.

"Who are you?" I asked.

"Frankie . . . P—" he slowly replied. "Frankie Pagoda."

He was in a lot of pain, and here's what was going on. His older brother, Scary Gary, who had already been in trouble with the law, had made him climb to the very top of a reedy Australian pine tree with a rope between his teeth. Then he tied the rope to the top of the tree and Gary tied the other end to the winch on Mr. Pagoda's tow truck. He winched the tip of the tree all the way down so it made a big spring and then Frankie held on like a Koala bear while Gary cut the rope with a machete. Frankie was launched like the stones the Romans flung at the Vandals.

I was in my bedroom and Mom was in the kitchen; both of us had windows that faced the backyard. Then we heard that first *Whoosh!* of the tree and Frankie hollering, "Ahhhhhh!" That was followed by a thud and a very soulful moan. And this is how we found him—on his back with his arms and legs slowly stretching out.

"Are you okay?" I asked. He slowly turned over onto his hands and knees.

"Yeah," he said, wincing. "I've had worse."

Mom pointed at him as if he were a garden pest. "He's a heap of trouble," she said to me. Then she said to Frankie, "If you have to hurt yourself, please do it in your own yard."

He seemed to nod to that and I helped him up and he ran off. A few minutes later we heard, *Whoosh!* "Ahhhhh!" *Thud!* "Ugh!" He was back.

"Something is messed up with those people," Mom said, chopping up onions that evening. "Something's wrong in their heads."

Maybe there was something wrong with me, too. I was different from Frankie but still, the first moment I saw him in pain, it occurred to me that I wanted to be in pain, too.

That evening my mother came into my room. "If I ever catch you playing with that kid or over at their house, you will be in big trouble. This is just a *friendly* warning," she said.

"Why?" I asked. "He's a neighbor and will probably be a friend."

"You should not be friends with kids who are a danger to themselves and others."

I got some courage up and replied, "That's what I love about him."

She pointed a red finger at my chest. "You are a *follower*, not a *leader*," she said bluntly. "You are putty in the wrong hands. Don't get me wrong. You're a nice kid, but you are most definitely a follower."

I sort of knew this was true but I didn't want to admit it to her. Plus, a little of me still wanted to believe that I was strong, that I was my own man and a great leader.

But within a week I was Frankie's man, which was pretty scary because he was Gary's man, which made me low man on the totem pole—or pine tree. The first time Gary launched me, I hit a car. It was an old Mercury Cougar parked in their backyard. It didn't have any wheels and sat on its belly like a cat crouching to catch a bird. I hit the roof, which was like a steel trampoline. It dented down and popped up and I went springing off the top. As I was in the air, I kept thinking, *When you hit the ground, roll and tumble and it won't hurt so much.* This is what I had learned from watching *Roller Derby* on TV. It was my favorite show and very violent, but the players always avoided massive debilitating and life-threatening injuries as long as they rolled and tumbled across the wooden track or over the rails and into the rows of metal folding chairs. So, as I flew through the air, I stared at the grassy yard and planned my clever descent. I hit the ground with my outstretched arms and, instead of bouncing as if my hands were shock absorbers, I collapsed into the ground like a piece of space junk.

I dislocated the fingers on my right hand, bruised the side of my face, and sprained my right shoulder. I limped home hunched over like Quasimodo and went straight to my room. A few minutes later I was barking in pain from relocating the joints in my fingers. I was so afraid my mother would see my bruised face that I stole my sister's makeup and powered my bruise. At dinner I couldn't use my right arm. It hung limply by my side like an elephant's trunk. I must have pinched a nerve on contact with the ground that left my arm paralyzed. Perhaps for life. I ate with my left hand and food kept falling down my chin and shirt and onto my lap.

"What's wrong with your arm?" my mother asked.

"Nothing," I mumbled.

She sneered, stood up, and came around to my side. She grabbed my arm and pulled on it like it was the starter rope on a lawnmower engine. Something deep inside my shoulder went *Pop!*

"Arghhh," I sighed. The relief from the pain was heavenly.

"You are as dumb as a post," my mother said. "I'm warning you—don't play with that kid! He'll lead you to your death."

I couldn't help myself. The next day I felt pretty good and my teeth no longer throbbed when I breathed through my mouth. As soon as my mother went into the bathroom I ran over to Frankie's house. His brother Gary had rigged up an electric chair with a train transformer. He ran copper leads from the transformer to chicken wire on the chair seat and duct-taped it down.

"Don't be a chicken," he said demonically when he saw me. "Take a seat."

I did and it was torture at its most challenging. When I got home I looked at my naked butt in the mirror, and it was singed with the same chicken wire pattern that was on the chair. "Wow," I said. "Pretty cool."

The next day my mother did the laundry. She came to me with my pants, which were singed with the same wire pattern. "You don't have to tell me how this happened," she said. "You just have to stop. Whatever drives you to do this stuff is a sickness. So I'm grounding you for a while until you start displaying some sense."

Maybe I was sick. Maybe I was a follower. But I couldn't help myself. I wanted to sneak back for more. I was just thinking of crawling out the window when I looked over at the Pagoda house, and Frankie had his bike up on the peak of his roof. He was poised to pedal down the slope and land in the pool, which was quite a distance from the eaves of the house.

"Go!" Gary demanded. Frankie did. He pedaled as fast as he could and yelled all the way down and then was in the air. My vision was blocked by a bush, and instead of a splashing sound there was the springy metal sound of his bike hitting the concrete patio and clattering around. In a minute Gary was hollering at him to stop being a sissy and to get up and the dent in his forehead wasn't anything to cry over. I rubbed my hand over my fore-head. *Perhaps a little dent of my own would look good*, I thought.

The ambulance arrived in a few minutes. After some begging, Mom allowed me to visit Frankie in the hospital, and later, once Scary Gary was sent off to a special program for dangerous boys, I even snuck over to Frankie's house a few times. He recovered just fine. And because he stopped doing dumb things for Gary, I stopped doing dumb things for him. He was a follower too, like me. And when you put two followers together nothing really bad happens. We didn't get hurt for a while or do anything too stu-pid. About a month went by before I secretly hoped Scary Gary would return home and rescue us from being so dull. I was bored out of my mind.

Biography:
Grew up: Mount Pleasant, Pennsylvania, then Barbados, then Florida

Now lives: Boston, Massachusetts

Random fact: Decided to write in sixth grade when he read his sister's diary and figured he could write better than she did

Selected Bibliography:
The Joey Pigza books
Jack Adrift: Fourth Grade without a Clue
Hole in My Life

DAVID MACAULAY
The Red Fire Engine

Bolton, Lancashire, England (1955 I think).

What I remember most clearly is how it felt. I'd just finished painting a red fire engine—like the one I often walked past near my grandparents' house. Suddenly the teachers, whose names I've long forgotten, closed in on my desk. They seemed unusually impressed, and my still-dripping fire engine was immediately and ceremoniously pinned up. I don't know what they might have said, but their unexpected attention and having something I'd made given a place of honor on the wall created an overwhelming and totally unfamiliar sense of pride inside me. I loved that feeling, and I wanted to feel it again and again. That desire, I suppose, was the beginning of my career.

I have no idea where my fire engine painting ended up, but I never forgot the basic layout. Several decades later, it served as the inspiration for this sketch for an illustration in a book called *Why the Chicken Crossed the Road*.

Biography:

Grew up: England, New Jersey, and Rhode Island. Completed the process in 1997.

Now lives: Bristol, Rhode Island—a blue state

Random fact: Was fifteen before he realized reading could be fun

Selected Bibliography:

The Way Things Work
Castle
Motel of the Mysteries

MORRIS GLEITZMAN
There Must Be a Mistake

"Dad," said the kids as we trundled around the supermarket. "Why do you keep moving your lips? Are you eating a fish finger on the sly?"

"Certainly not," I retorted, allowing a store detective to shine his torch inside my mouth so they could see it was empty. "I'm adding up the grocery prices in my head."

The kids looked at me, impressed. Well, not exactly impressed. More concerned. "Dad," they said. "You promised Mum you'd stop doing dopey male things to try and impress people."

I sighed. Women and children just don't understand what it's like to be a guy. To have these wonderful powers and to see the admiration in the faces of onlookers when you use them.

We arrived at the checkout. Before the girl had finished swiping our groceries I gave her thirty-six dollars and twenty-nine cents and waited for her to be impressed.

"That'll be a hundred and forty-two dollars," she said.

"Hang on," I said. "There must be a mistake. If there's three things I'm really good at it's soccer, knitting, Nintendo, and math."

The kids made me pay the hundred and forty-two dollars and we went to the fruit market where, amazingly, exactly the same thing happened.

"There you are," I said, slapping the right money into the storekeeper's hand. "Five pounds of not very ripe oranges at one twenty-nine a pound, that's four sixty-six."

The storekeeper shook his head.

"Don't try to tell me my math is wrong," I said.

"I'm not," said the storekeeper. "I'm trying to tell you these are avocados."

The kids made me pay the forty-four dollars and twenty-five cents.

"He undercharged me," I whispered gleefully as we left the shop. "Fifteen times two ninety-five is sixty-eight dollars. I've just made thirty-two fifty."

"Good," muttered the kids. "Use it to buy a calculator."

I did better than that. In the discount electronics store the calculators were only twelve ninety-five, so I gave my profit from the fruit market to the checkout person and took two.

Biography:

Grew up: Sleaford, Lincolnshire, England, and farther south in suburbs of London, then Australia

Now lives: Melbourne, Australia

Random fact: Eats more spinach than any other children's author in the southern hemisphere

Selected Bibliography:

Toad Rage
Toad Heaven
Worry Warts

DAVID GRANGER
Thwacked

In eighth grade, there was this kid named David. He was sitting in math class. His math teacher was a really attractive young woman. He'd been doing push-ups and sit-ups quite a bit of late. There might not have been a connection between the fact that his teacher was pretty and the fact that he was doing push-ups and sit-ups quite a bit, though he did sit next to Debbie Belitsos in history, and she might have contributed to his push-ups and sit-ups, too.

There were a bunch of kids in David's math class, but only one of them had decided to torment David on that day. A skinny kid named Bill Dugan. You know that thing you can do with the fingers of your right hand? You put the tips of your first and third fingers on something and you pull your middle finger back against your palm with your thumb and then you flick whatever it is your fingertips are on (a table, a window, someone's head) with the middle finger. You can get a good *thwack!* out of that flick. It hurts your middle finger, not to mention whatever it is you thwack.

So Bill Dugan, every time he walked by this kid David in math class, would thwack him on the back of the head. He did it, like, three or four or five times this day and it created a predicament for David. In a few ways. First, it hurt. Second, it was humiliating to be thwacked on the back of the head by this kid. Third, Bill Dugan tended to hang out with a bunch of guys who included some guys who were big enough (for middle school kids) to be considered freakish. And they liked to pound on other kids. Fourth, it was particularly humiliating to be thwacked when you considered that the math teacher was kind of pretty.

You could tell that the math teacher had always thought this kid David was a nice kid. He was a decent student and he talked in class and he didn't hate math. So she was really surprised when she turned around from facing the blackboard. She turned around because she'd heard a loud noise, and she discovered that the loud noise had been caused by Bill Dugan falling over a desk. Bill Dugan had fallen over the desk because right after he thwacked this kid David on the back of the head for the fourth or fifth or sixth time, this kid David stood up and hit him in the face—hit him in the face two or three or four times until he fell over the desk that then made the loud noise that made the math teacher turn around. You could tell that the math teacher had thought David was a nice kid because as she began to understand what had happened—at least to the degree that Bill Dugan was on the floor and David had put him there—you could see her expression change from surprise to alarm to disappointment. You could see that she wouldn't ever think of this kid David in the same way again.

By this time, Bill Dugan was bleeding a little bit, and the kid named David was crying a little bit. The two of them had to go to the vice principal's office. They had to sit outside his door together while they waited, and you can guess that was weird. I mean, they'd just had a fight and now they had to sit on the same bench, practically touching, until the vice principal made time for them. Eventually, he opened his door and told them to come in and asked them *What's this all about?* This had to be the worst part, for a few reasons. First, it's always tough being bawled out by the vice principal. Second, they had to be figuring that the vice principal was going to call their parents. Third, it's hard to tell your version of events when you're sitting in the vice principal's office and you're worried about your parents finding out and you're mad at yourself because you feel like you might start crying again.

But eventually, the vice principal seemed to gather enough evidence, and he talked to them both very sternly about the proper way for men to handle disagreements, which seemed kind of weird, because the only thing they'd disagreed on was whether it was enjoyable for this kid David to get thwacked on the head. And after a while the vice principal told them to stand up. And he said, "David Granger, Bill Dugan, I want you to shake hands." And that was it. And I have to say that it was pretty clear to everyone that this kid David thought he'd gotten a pretty good deal.

Biography:
Grew up: California, Massachusetts, Kentucky, and Tennessee
Now lives: Outside New York City
Random fact: Always liked lima beans
Occupation: Editor in Chief, *Esquire* magazine

DAN GREENBURG
My Superpowers

Do you ever wish you had superpowers?

When I was a kid, growing up on the North Side of Chicago and being picked on by bullies, I prayed for superpowers. Like Superman, I wanted to be able to fly faster than speeding bullets, to be more powerful than locomotives, to leap tall buildings at a single bound. Mainly, I wanted to punch bullies in the stomach so hard that my fist came out of their backs.

Winters in Chicago are so cold that frost forms leafy patterns on your bedroom window and stays there for months. The wind howls off Lake Michigan, and a thick shell of pitted black ice covers the streets and sidewalks from December to April. To keep warm in winter, I wore a heavy wool coat, a wool muffler, wool mittens, furry earmuffs and—one of my most treasured possessions—a Chicago Cubs baseball cap autographed by a player named Big Bill Nicholson.

On the coldest days of winter, three bullies waited for me after school, just for the fun of terrorizing me. The biggest one was a fat ugly kid named Vernon Manteuffel. Vernon and his two buddies would pull off my Cubs cap and tease me with it. They'd pretend to give it back, then toss it around in a game of keep-away.

One day in February when the temperature was so low I felt my eyeballs cracking, Vernon and his friends caught up with me on my way home. As usual, they tore off my Cubs cap and started playing catch with it. What made it worse than usual was that on this particular day I happened to be walking home with a pretty girl named Ann Cohn, who lived across the street from me. Ann Cohn had green eyes and shiny black hair and I had a goofy crush on her. As if it wasn't bad enough that these guys humiliated me when I was alone, now they were doing it in front of Ann Cohn.

I was so embarrassed, I began to cry. Crying in front of Ann Cohn made me even more embarrassed. I was speechless with shame and anger. Driven by rage, I did what only an insane person would do: I attacked Vernon Manteuffel. I punched him in the chest and grabbed back my Cubs cap.

Vernon saw that I had become a madman. People don't know what to do with madmen. Vernon looked shocked and even a little afraid. He backed away from me. I attacked the second boy, who also backed away from me. Encouraged by their backing away, I ran after them, screaming, punching, flailing at them with both fists. I chased them for two blocks before they finally pulled ahead and disappeared. Breathing hard, tears streaming down my face, I felt I had regained my honor, at least temporarily.

That weekend, perhaps made braver by my triumph over the three bullies, I kissed Ann Cohn on her sofa. I can't tell you exactly why I did that. Maybe because it was a cold, cloudy Saturday and there was nothing else to do. Maybe because we both wondered what it would feel like. In any case, I could now brag that, at age eight, I had personally kissed an actual girl who wasn't related to me.

I never did get those superpowers. Not as a kid, at least.

When I grew up, I became a writer. I discovered a particular pleasure in going on risky adventures. I wrote about my real-life adventures for national magazines: I spent four months riding with New York firefighters and running into burning buildings with them. I spent six months riding with New York homicide cops as they chased and captured drug dealers and murderers. I flew upside-down over the Pacific Ocean with a stunt pilot in an open-cockpit airplane. I took part in dangerous voodoo ceremonies in Haiti. I spent time on a tiger ranch in Texas and learned to tame two-hundred-pound tigers by yelling "*No!*" and smacking them hard on the nose. I found that tigers were not much different from the bullies of my childhood in Chicago.

I also wrote fiction. I created entire worlds and filled them with people I wanted to put in there. I made these people do and say whatever it pleased me to have them do and say. In the worlds I made up, I was all-powerful—*I had superpowers.*

I began writing a series of children's books called The Zack Files, about a boy named Zack who keeps stumbling into the supernatural. In many of these books I gave Zack temporary powers—to read minds, to travel outside his body, to travel back into the past, to triumph over ghosts and monsters. I created another series called Maximum Boy, about a boy named Max who accidentally touches radioactive rocks that just came back from outer space and who suddenly develops super powers. Maximum Boy is me as a kid in Chicago, but with superpowers.

Oh yeah, I almost forgot. In The Zack Files, I created a fat, stupid kid who sweats a lot and thinks he's cool, but who everyone laughs at behind his back. You know what I named this fool? Vernon Manteuffel. I do hope the real Vernon knows.

Biography:

Grew up: Chicago, Illinois
Now lives: North of New York City on the Hudson River
Random fact: Writing is his favorite activity

Selected Bibliography:

How I Became a Superhero (Maximum Boy #1)
Superhero . . . or Super Thief? (Maximum Boy #3)
Tell a Lie and Your Butt Will Grow (The Zack Files #28)

ANDY GRIFFITHS
My Dad Is Better Than Your Dad

"My dad's better than your dad," says Buck.

"No he's not," I say.

"Yes he is," says Buck. "He's tougher for a start."

"Yeah, right," I say. "My dad's a black belt. Can't get much tougher than that."

"Yes you can," says Buck. "My dad's a double black belt."

"No such thing," I say.

"There is so," says Buck. "He beat up ten blokes once. With his bare hands."

"My dad beat up fifty blokes," I say. "With his hands tied behind his back."

"My dad beat up three thousand blokes," says Buck. "And he was completely frozen inside a block of ice."

"Big deal," I say. "My dad's been inside a volcano. While it was erupting. Wearing nothing but a pair of underpants."

"So what?" says Buck. "My dad's been to the moon—without a space suit!"

"Space travel?" I say. "That is *so* boring. My dad's got a time machine. He went back to the Jurassic age and fought a Tyrannosaurus."

Buck snorts. "My dad reckons time machines are for kids. He prefers driving his Porsche."

"My dad's got a Porsche, too," I say. "In fact, my dad is so rich his Porsche has got a Porsche. He's a billionaire, you know."

"Only a billionaire?" says Buck. "My dad's a zillionaire!"

"Oh, did I say billionaire?" I say. "I meant krillionaire."

"Krillionaire?" says Buck. "There's no such thing."

"You've never heard of a krillionaire?" I say. "Gee, I'd hate to be so poor that I didn't know what a krillionaire is. You know all those tiny shrimp things that whales eat? They're called krill. Well, my dad gets his satellite to scan the ocean and he sees all these countless krill in the water and because they're countless he uses that to describe how many dollars he has because he has so many that it's impossible to count them all."

"Oh really?" says Buck. "Your dad is still working with outdated technology that can't count all the krill in the ocean? My dad's satellite can see in so much detail that he is capable of not only counting all the krill in the ocean but identifying each krill individually and giving a name to each one. But krillions are nothing to him. Krillions is just a word he uses for his spare change. He's so rich he owns practically everything on earth."

"My dad *owns* the earth," I say. "In fact, he owns the whole solar system."

"He doesn't own it," says Buck. "He just *rents* it. From my dad. My dad owns the entire universe. All the stars. All the asteroids. All the UFOs. All the black holes. Everything. You name it, my dad owns it."

He stands there with his hands on his hips. Smirking.

I shrug.

This is not over yet.

Not by a long shot.

"That may be so," I say, "but my dad can wiggle his ears!"

Buck groans.

He knows as well as I do that you can own all the universe

you want, but if you can't wiggle your ears, what's the point?

Now it's my turn to put my hands on my hips. "Well? Got anything to say?"

"Yeah," says Buck. "My mom is better than your mom."

Biography:

Grew up: Melbourne, Australia
Now lives: Melbourne, Australia
Random fact: His dad can wiggle his ears

Selected Bibliography:

The Day My Butt Went Psycho
Just Stupid!
Just Wacky!

ADAM McCAULEY

When I was a kid, I read a lot. The first books I really got into were the Wizard of Oz books by L. Frank Baum. I loved the stories and the creatures, like the Wheelies and Tik-Tok and the Nome King. I also loved the fantastic illustrations by John R. Neill. When I got a little older, I read *The Hobbit* and *The Lord of the Rings*, by J. R. R. Tolkien. I loved to draw the characters and scenes from the books, and I was also inspired to create my own alphabets and languages.

My older brother Kevin was an amazing artist, and he read a lot of history books and did paintings of people like Joan of Arc and Henry VIII. He also made funny comics about his adventures playing Dungeons and Dragons. The comic book on the next page, which he made when he was about seventeen is based on the Conan the Barbarian books, by Robert E. Howard, which he loved.

Of course, I tried to be just as good an artist, so I copied him by drawing the same kinds of subjects, such as an evil warrior showing a knight who's the boss. I think I was around ten or eleven when I drew that. My parents had an illustrated version of *The Canterbury Tales*, by Geoffrey Chaucer, which also inspired me to draw the amazing costumes of that period.

As I got older I enjoyed reading science fiction stories. I did the second drawing when I was about fifteen. It's of a Kzinti, a giant catlike alien from the book *Ringworld*, by Larry Niven. Now that I'm an old guy, I still love to read and draw—like for Jon Scieszka's hilarious Time Warp Trio books!

Biography:

Grew up: Portland, Oregon; Columbia, Missouri; Ethiopia; and Palo Alto, California

Now lives: San Francisco, California

Random fact: Loves to play his set of Gretsch drums

Selected Bibliography:

The Time Warp Trio by Jon Scieszka, books 9–14

My Friend Chicken

The Lima Bean Monster

Cover by Adam's brother Kevin.

An evil warrior showing a knight who's boss.

A *Kzinti from* Ringworld

DAN GUTMAN
Let's Go to the Videotape

I wasn't the skinniest boy in Newark, New Jersey.

Okay, well maybe I *was* the skinniest boy in Newark, New Jersey.

I have no proof either way. But kids at school used to say to me, "You're so skinny that when you go to the movies, you can't hold the seat down." Kids used to say, "Did you hear that Gutman disappeared? Yeah, he turned *sideways*."

Very funny.

Nowadays of course, everybody knows that it's *good* to be skinny, for health reasons. And now that I'm pushing fifty, I'm kind of glad that I've always been thin.

But back in 1965, I was ashamed and humiliated that I could just about put my hand around my own ribs. My legs were like matchsticks. Clothes never fit me right. The waistband of my pants, for some reason, seemed to naturally fall just below my armpits. I wouldn't wear a watch because even the smallest wristband would slide up and down my arm. I was short, too.

I was a mutant freak!

I tried to gain weight, I really did. I heard that drinking milk shakes and eating bananas would make you bulk up. So I tried it. I didn't gain a pound. What can I say? I never had a big appetite. To this day, I eat a couple of bites of food and feel full.

Finally, in fourth or fifth grade, I decided to do something about it. I decided to try weights.

Not lifting them, mind you. That would have been too much work. I'm talking about putting weights in my *shoes*.

You see, my father had a printing business that he ran out of our basement. He had all these thin pieces of lead that he used to separate the lines of type.

One day each year at school, each class would be marched down to the nurse's office for the annual ritual of being weighed, measured, and (in my case) humiliated. It was no fun being the skinniest and shortest boy in the class.

So I hit on a great idea: I would borrow some of my dad's lead weights and slip them in my shoes to make myself heavier and taller. Nobody would know the difference.

No, they didn't. The lead added maybe one pound to my weight and a half an inch to my height. The kids still laughed at me. And it was hard to walk with all that lead in my shoes.

The worst part of school for me, naturally, was gym class. I was never good at sports. I didn't have the arm strength to climb the ropes in gym. I didn't have the endurance to run the mile. Baseball was always my favorite sport, but I couldn't hit the ball. I was always afraid the ball was going to hit *me*. (It never did, but once I ran into a tree while chasing a Frisbee.)

The gym teacher at Mt. Vernon School was Mr. Feely (yes, that was his real name). He made us play basketball a lot. When things got rough, I was always the one on the floor, getting trampled by the other players.

The worst possible words out of Mr. Feely—to me, anyway—were, "Okay boys, shirts and skins." The skins team, of course, had to take their shirts off. At least with a shirt on, I didn't look *too* much like a walking skeleton.

I would pray, *Please put me on the shirt team. Please put me on the shirt team.*

"Gutman!" Mr. Feely would always bellow. "You're a skin."

But usually, the game we played in gym was kickball. I liked kickball, mostly because nobody had to take off his shirt to play it.

There were about a dozen boys on each team, and the fielders would scatter across the big gym. Little guys like me would try to hit dribblers past the infield and scoot to first base before the ball got there. Big guys could bang the ball as far as they could and bounce it off the far wall.

There was one game I will never forget as long as I live. My team was "at bat." We sat in a line on the side waiting our turn to kick. Edmund Fortuna was sitting next to me. He turned to me and said, "Hey, Gutman, do you realize you're the only guy on the team who isn't wearing Cons?"

"Cons" were Converse All-Stars, those canvas sneakers that were state-of-the-art in the sixties (this was before Nike and Adidas came along).

I looked down the line, and Edmund was right. Every single kid except for me was wearing Cons. I had cheap, no-name sneakers. Suddenly, I felt ashamed. Ashamed of my stupid sneakers.

It was my turn to kick and I was mad. I decided that instead of trying for my usual cheap single, I would just whack the ball with everything I had. That's what I did.

The ball took off and sailed across the gym, straight as an arrow. I headed for first, keeping my eye on the ball to see where it would land. It looked like it had a chance to reach the far wall, or at least the basketball backboard that was attached to the wall. If it bounced off the backboard, that would make it doubly hard to catch.

The ball was on a downward trajectory when I reached first. Kids had positioned themselves under the backboard in case the ball didn't reach it.

And that's when it happened.

The ball went through the hoop!

Swish. Nothing but net. I had kicked a basket all the way across the gym!

Everybody stopped. It was like the Day the Earth Stood Still. Nobody had *ever* kicked a basket before. We didn't know what to do.

"Home run!" Mr. Feely announced. "That's a thousand runs!"

I circled the bases triumphantly. Then I sat back down next to Edmund Fortuna.

"Let's see you and your Cons do *that*," I said.

When we got back to class, everybody was talking about what happened in gym class. "Gutman kicked a basket! Gutman kicked a basket!" As the girls heard the news, they were looking at me with new respect. I was working hard to act like it was no big deal.

This incident happened nearly forty years ago, but I remember it like it was five minutes ago. I'm sure that none of the other guys who were there that day remember it at all. It was only important to *me*.

It would be nice to say that this was the beginning of my incredible athletic career, the turning point where I went from being a skinny little geek who couldn't play sports into a real jock. Stories are supposed to have happy endings, right?

Well, forget it. I'm still a skinny little geek who can't play sports.

But sometimes, when I'm lying in bed at night before I fall asleep, I roll this mental videotape I have of the time I kicked a basket in gym class. In my mind, I watch myself kick that basket over and over again.

I'll bet every kid has at least one of those moments in his life when he did something really, really great, something really unexpected.

Close your eyes and think of that moment from time to time. Remember it just the way it happened. Never let that video fade away. Someday, forty years from now, when you're lying in bed at night, you might want to replay it.

Biography:

Grew up: Newark, New Jersey

Now lives: Haddonfield, New Jersey

Random fact: Thinks baseball is better than any other sport because it's the most complex

Selected Bibliography:

Jackie & Me

The Kid Who Became President

Miss Daisy Is Crazy! (My Weird School #1) illustrated by Jim Paillot

BRUCE HALE
Boys, Beer, Barf, and Bonding

At first, I thought the whole thing was kinda dorky. I mean, wearing uniforms, tying knots, and helping old ladies cross the street? I had my doubts about Boy Scouts.

What's worse, my dad—Mr. Ex-Marine, Mr. Spit-and-Polish—was scoutmaster. Scary? Let's just say I had to keep reminding myself that he was my dad.

All in all, Boy Scouts looked to be as much fun as yanking out your molars with a rusty pair of pliers.

But then I discovered what our troop was really all about: gnarly guys out in the wilderness. Each month, we'd hit the high Sierras. There we hiked, fished, farted, ate chili-macaroni, and just generally went without bathing.

This was cool. This was manliness. I started to like Boy Scouts.

One summer, we planned a long-term hike. Seven days of tramping the backcountry, with no moms, no soft beds—just gnarly guys. I was only twelve, but I could almost feel whiskers sprouting on my chin.

"This'll be great!" I told my friend Billy.

"Awesome!" he agreed.

The day came, and everyone piled into station wagons. Countless rounds of "99 Bottles of Beer" later, we reached the trailhead, parked, and set off.

Day after day, our packs grew heavier, and our blisters multiplied. But we toughed it out. We learned manly skills like cleaning fish and putting out a campfire by whizzing on it.

Through it all, my semi-scary dad led the way. We weren't exactly buddy-buddy, but he kept an eye on me.

By the fourth day, Billy and I had serious food cravings. Visions of ice cream and hamburgers and pizza filled our thoughts. We weren't homesick; we were just sick of fish and chili-macaroni.

Finally, the last day arrived. Filthy and footsore, our troop stumbled out of the trailhead and into its cars.

On the drive back, no one sang "99 Bottles of Beer." Everyone chanted McDonald's and Burger King songs.

We would not be denied.

In L.A., we stopped at a burger joint for the porkout to end all porkouts. Mountains of hamburgers, piles of fries, and lakes of milk shakes poured down our gullets. We ate until our guts ached. Pure bliss.

Then we crawled into our cars, stuffed, like pythons digesting a whole cow. Ten minutes from home, a sudden cramp racked my belly.

"Oooh, I don't feel so hot."

"We're almost there," said my dad.

As we dropped off Billy and his father, my insides burbled and shifted. Uh-oh. "Dad . . ."

He rubbed his gut. "I feel it, too," he said. "Hang on. Just one more block."

We whipped around the corner and into the driveway. Bent double, we staggered to the front door. Locked.

And Mom's car was gone.

"Don't you have the key?" I asked.

"Thought she'd be home," said my dad. "Check the back door."

My guts were churning like molten lava. I shuffled around back, thighs clamped tight. Another locked door.

"Dad, what do we do?"

"Maybe the balcony door is open."

I eyed the second-floor balcony. On a good day, I could scale it, no problem. On a good day.

"Up you go," said my dad. He headed into the backyard.

I groaned. The lava was bubbling. This volcano could blow at any second. Somehow, I climbed the bushes, flung a leg over the railing, and stepped onto the balcony.

I tried the door.

"It's locked!" I cried.

"Fend for yourself!" my dad shouted.

And just then, the volcano exploded.

Blaaaargh! I erupted from both ends. Burgers, fries, milk shake and all made a reappearance.

Blaaargh! came the answering call from the backyard, where Dad was having an eruption of his own.

Fifteen minutes too late, my mom pulled into the drive-way. After helping us get cleaned up, she asked, "Did you have a good time?"

Dad and I shared a look.

"Not bad," I said. "Not bad at all." And in that moment, strangely, I felt closer to my dad than I ever had before.

Biography:

Grew up: Raised by wolves just outside Los Angeles, California

Now lives: Santa Barbara, California

Random fact: Is also an actor, who played a surfer's agent in an independent movie called *The Ride*

Selected Bibliography:

The Malted Falcon (A Chet Gecko Mystery)
Trouble Is My Beeswax (A Chet Gecko Mystery)
The Hamster of the Baskervilles (A Chet Gecko Mystery)

Biography:

Grew up: Berkshire, England

Now lives: The Isle of Oxney (not an island), Kent, England

Random fact: When Dave was a kid, he saw *The Spy Who Loved Me*, and from then on he always wanted a Lotus Esprit as driven by James Bond underwater. When he did his first stupid advertising job (for Sony PlayStation), he bought one. Sadly, it doesn't turn into a submarine.

Selected Bibliography:

Coraline by Neil Gaiman

The Day I Swapped My Dad for 2 Goldfish with Neil Gaiman

The Wolves in the Walls by Neil Gaiman

DANIEL HANDLER
Principals and Principles

In San Francisco the weather never gets hot, and when it does it lasts only three days. On the first day, the hot weather is a surprise, and everyone wanders around carrying their sweaters. On the second day, everyone enjoys the heat. And on the third day, the cold weather returns and is just as surprising, and everyone wanders around shivering.

One of these three-day heat waves arrived when I was in seventh grade, and on the first day everyone was grumpy because we had all dressed for fog and gloom and now had to drag our sweaters all over the school. We all agreed that the next day we'd dress for warm weather, but just as the day ended, the principal made an announcement over the loudspeaker. "Students at Herbert Hoover Middle School are not allowed to wear shorts," she said, in the tone of voice she always used—a tone of voice that sounded friendly but was actually unbearably wicked.

Everyone groaned—everyone but me. "She can't do that," I said, and reached into the back of my binder. On the first day of school, we'd all received a pamphlet: "Student Rights and Responsibilities." For some reason I'd saved it, and I read one of our rights out loud: "Students have the right to free dress." I convinced everyone to wear shorts the next day in order to protest the wicked principal's unfair cancellation of one of our rights.

The next day was wonderful because we were all dressed for the heat and nobody had to drag their sweaters around, but of course, I was sent to the principal's office—someone had ratted on me. (To this day, I suspect Nancy Cutler, but I can't prove it.) She asked me if I had told everyone to wear shorts. I said yes. She said shorts were distracting to some of the teachers. I said that free dress was one of our rights. She said that shorts led students to have water fights. I said that free dress was one of our rights. She said that she was the principal and she was in charge. I said that free dress was one our rights. She kept pointing at me. I kept pointing at the pamphlet. The principal was one of those people who yelled at you until you cried, but I forced myself not to cry, biting my lip and blinking very, very fast, until at last she gave up and I was allowed to return to my classmates, who applauded me. In celebration, we all wore shorts the next day, too, even though we knew the cold weather would return, and it did, and we were shivering and miserable.

In eighth grade we got a new version of the pamphlet. Instead of "Students have the right to free dress," it read, "Students have the responsibility to dress appropriately." I threw it away.

If you stand up for your rights, you can count on the fact that the wicked people will find sneaky ways to change the rules. But you should stand up for your rights anyway, because there aren't enough sunny days in the world, and everyone should enjoy them.

Biography:

Grew up: By the seashore

Now lives: By the skin of his teeth

Random fact: Has eaten rotten shark, which is considered a delicacy in Iceland

Selected Bibliography:

A Series of Unfortunate Events books illustrated by Brett Helquist • *Lemony Snicket: The Unauthorized Autobiography*

WILL HOBBS
A Great, Big, Beautiful World

My two older brothers and I ran in a pack. One of my earliest memories is rounding up box turtles from the woods behind our house in Falls Church, Virginia. We kept them only three days. Catch and release, I guess you could call it. When my brothers learned that some kids down the street were keeping two dozen box turtles, we were outraged. We sneaked into their backyard—when they weren't home, naturally. We let all their turtles go. At the age of four, this made quite an impression on me. Don't try this at home!

We were an air force family. Next up was Alaska with its mountains and rivers and bears. By now we had a little sister and brother in tow. Baseball was big. A couple of times we played by the midnight sun. I got hooked on fishing down on the Kenai River, an amazing turquoise gem loaded with trout and salmon. I fell in love with rivers and was in awe of the bear tracks in the mud. During fourth grade, reading grabbed hold of my imagination and took it on one adventure after another. *Call It Courage* was my first favorite book.

We left Alaska on a navy ship in January of '58. A huge winter storm in the Gulf of Alaska turned us every way but loose. We landed green in the gills in northern California. Terra Linda was a kids' paradise: Little League, paper route, Scouts, and open hillsides to explore. For sixth grade I had the coolest teacher, Mr. Pilch. He knew that I spent a good deal of time looking for gopher snakes, king snakes, and alligator lizards, so he kept a terrarium in the classroom and let me stock it with a snake of the month.

Reptiles came first, but any sort of critter fascinated me, even skunks. When my cousin was visiting, we cornered one against the water tower just to see what would happen. We ran home in a state of high reek. My mother thought we were amusing.

Cardboard sledding was also high on my list. All summer, the wild oats on the hillsides were slick as could be, and they made for thrilling rides on huge flat pieces of cardboard we would cut from refrigerator boxes. Miraculously, no one was maimed.

My baseball career peaked when I struck out the side once on nine pitches. We were huge Giants fans. Our dad took us often to see Number 24 play—the "Say-Hey Kid," Willie Mays.

California, with our Scout troop, was where I first started backpacking, on treks in the high Sierras. We moved to San Antonio, Texas, for my high school years, but I was lucky enough to work four summers as a guide at Philmont Scout Ranch in New Mexico during late high school and college. During my most memorable summer, I had a horse and burros, and packed in supplies to a remote camp where I led kids into a long-abandoned gold mine. At the end of the summer I would head back to the Sierras with a brother or friend for backpacking along the John Muir Trail, thirteen days once without resupply.

Wilderness had become such a big part of me; I lived from one adventure to the next. I talked my little brother into a ten-day canoe trip on the Bowron Lakes chain in British Columbia. It was rainy, and a two-dollar tube tent didn't serve us well. My meal planning wasn't so great either. We'd live off fish, I told my brother, and supplement it with granola. Well, we proved that you can live off granola for ten days.

When I got married and moved to Colorado, I became even more dedicated to spending time in the wild places. Jean loved where a backpack could take her, and so did our nieces and nephews. I've done over thirty trips in the high country of the Weminuche wilderness, where my early books *Bearstone* and *Beardance* take place. We became serious river rats. We've been lucky enough to take our own raft through the Grand Canyon ten times so far, and that's why I had to write *Downriver*, to take my readers along.

The North keeps calling me back, to adventures in Canada's Yukon and Northwest Territories, and all over Alaska—sea kayaking, running rivers, working on a salmon troller. I just love being there, and sometimes, afterward, I start thinking of a story. I mined my personal experience heavily for *Far North*, *Wild Man Island*, and *Leaving Protection*.

There's a character in one of my books who says, "Life is best lived as an adventure," and you can see where he got that. It's still a great, big, beautiful world out there. Enjoy it; take care of it!

Biography:

Grew up: Pennsylvania, Panama, Virginia, Alaska, northern and southern California, and Texas

Now lives: Durango, Colorado

Random fact: Built two of his own houses from the ground up

Selected Bibliography:

Jason's Gold
Far North
The Maze

ANTHONY HOROWITZ
My French Teacher Tried to Kill Me

When I was twelve years old, my French teacher tried to kill me. It was my own fault. I'd followed him back to the staff room after class and had listened as he made a private telephone call to a number in Berlin. That was when I had discovered that he wasn't a French teacher at all. Marco-Pierre St. John Robson was actually an international assassin, pretending to be a French teacher. . . . And what better place than a shabby private school in a quiet corner of North London?

I'd always suspected it. Those gray, ugly eyes. The rubbery skin. The sheer amount of hair in his nostrils. No teacher could really be that ugly. And what about the oversized hearing aid he was always wearing? It had to be some sort of radio receiver, beaming in his latest instructions.

The bad news was that he'd seen me following him. He knew that I knew, and he couldn't risk anyone else finding out. The next day in class, I saw him walking purposefully toward me, trying to look normal. But now I realized it was just an act. He leaned over my shoulder, pretending to examine my work, and I heard him whisper in my ear, "*Au revoir*, Monsieur Horowitz. You should not have meddled in my affairs." At the same time, out of the corner of my eye, I saw six inches of pointed steel on some sort of hidden mechanism slide out of his sleeve. He intended to finish me, right now, in the middle of French dictation.

I only had one chance. There was a bottle of ink on my desk and the lid was off. Casually, I reached out and took hold of it, then flicked my hand backward. The ink splattered over his face and into his eyes, momentarily blinding him. In the same instant, I rolled my feet up and kicked against the desk. The back of my chair crashed into his stomach, and as he doubled over, I lashed upward, driving my fist into his . . .

Of course, none of this is true. But this is the dream I used to dream in just about every French lesson. I'd let the sound of Mr. Robson and his subjunctive verbs fade into the background, and for a moment I'd forget that I was lonely, unhappy, and bottom of the class. And later on, in geography, I'd grapple with Miss Buxtead, who was quite obviously an alien who intended to suck my brains out with a straw if I let her. And then, in math, it would be the turn of Mr. Priestley, who had no reflection when he went past a mirror and who, I was certain, never went out in the sunlight. . . .

And now? My French isn't up to much. I can't tell you the capital of Ethiopia and couldn't work out how long it would take me to get there. But if you ask me what it was like to be a guy . . . well, for me, doing badly at school was part of the answer.

I hated school. But I still enjoy the dreams.

Biography:

Grew up: Stanmore, Middlesex, England (near London)
Now lives: Crouch End, North London
Random fact: Had a dog called Lucky but accidentally ran it over, so he changed the dog's name to Unlucky

Selected Bibliography:

Eagle Strike (An Alex Rider Adventure)
Skeleton Key (An Alex Rider Adventure)
Stormbreaker (An Alex Rider Adventure)

JAMES HOWE
Learning How to Be a Boy

Today in gym Kevin Hennessey called me a girl. I reminded him that we're trying to stop name-calling in our school, and he said, "I'm not calling you a name, faggot, I'm calling you a girl, which you are." I didn't even bother to point out that "faggot" is a name. What is the point? Kevin Hennessey has an IQ smaller than his neck size. Actually, he has a head smaller than his neck size. I'm so not kidding.

Well, I'm used to being called a girl, but, excuse me, is that supposed to be an insult? What's wrong with girls? Some of my best friends are girls! But I know what Kevin H. and all the other (um, no name-calling, so you'll have to use your imagination here) _____s mean when they say it. They mean I'm not a boy.

Okay, fine, I'm not a boy like them, but I'm still a boy. The thing is, boys—by which I mean guy-guys like my brother Jeff—have always been a total mystery to me. I mean, how do they know how to do all that stuff like throw and catch and grease car engines? Besides the fact that I don't have a clue how to do any of those things, on a scale of one to ten, I have, like, below zero interest. Way below. Try negative a thousand.

If they didn't spend so much time trying to make my life miserable, I'd actually feel sorry for guy-guys. I mean, they must get so tired of having to spit and fart and act tough all the time.

Okay, here's the part that's hard for me to admit: as much as I don't understand guy-guys—and sometimes actually feel sorry for them—I went through a period in my life when I wanted to be one. I kept thinking there was something wrong with me for not knowing how to, I don't know, be a boy. I don't know why, but all of a sudden in the fifth grade I wanted to be a guy-guy so badly that I actually asked my friend Skeezie to teach me how. It was pathetic.

Skeezie: Stop crossing your legs at the knee.

Me: What does that have to do with being a guy-guy?

Skeezie: It has to do with guys do not cross their legs at the knee. Your aunt Priscilla crosses her legs at the knee.

Me: I don't have an aunt Priscilla. Although I wish I did. I love the name.

Skeezie: You're an aunt Priscilla, OK? Now listen up, and do what I'm tellin' ya. If you gotta cross your legs, you keep one leg at a right angle to the floor and put your other ankle on the knee of that leg. Like this.

Me: Oh my god, you look just like that gangster in that movie. You know, the one with Al Pacino and all the blood?

Skeezie: Do it!

Me: Ow. It hurts.

Skeezie: Stop waving your hands around.

Me: I'm not waving—

Skeezie: Yes, you are. Guys don't wave their hands around. They keep their hands quiet.

Me: Well, that's boring.

Skeezie: What are you doing?

Me: What?

Skeezie: Your hands. You're folding them in your lap.

Me: I'm keeping them quiet.

Skeezie: Your aunt Priscilla sits with her hands folded in her lap.

Me: Not with her legs crossed like this, she doesn't. Where are you going?

Skeezie: I give up, Joe. Just be who you are, OK?

Me: But you haven't taught me how to talk sports yet. How 'bout them Yankees, huh, Skeezie? How 'bout them Yankees?

Skeezie never did teach me how to talk sports. And he didn't teach me how to be a guy-guy. But he did teach me how to be a boy. "Just be who you are, OK?" That's what he said; you heard him. Well, I am a boy—even if I don't spit and fart and act tough. So what if I sit more like my aunt Priscilla than some gangster in a movie I can't remember the name of?

The next time Kevin Hennessey says I'm a girl, I'll have to point out that he seems to be suffering from gender confusion. Luckily for me, he won't have a clue what I'm talking about. He'll probably just spit and call me a faggot. Oh, well, Kevin is a guy-guy, after all. His options are limited.

"Learning How to Be a Boy" is adapted from the novel *Totally Joe* by James Howe to be published by Simon & Schuster in Fall 2005.

Biography:

Grew up: Webster, New York

Now lives: Yonkers, New York

Random fact: Used to want to be a horse jockey (but is 6'2")

Selected Bibliography:

Bunnicula with Deborah Howe

The Celery Stalks at Midnight

The Misfits

Jarrett J. Krosoczka, Lightning Man, part 1: age 9

Biography **Grew up:** Worcester, Massachusetts **Now lives:** Boston **Random fact:** Works on the same drafting table today that he did when he was fourteen. (It was a birthday present from his grandparents.) **Selected Bibliography** *Bubble Bath Pirates!* • *Baghead* • *Punk Farm*

Jarrett J. Krosoczka, Lightning Man, part 2: age 26

BRIAN JACQUES
A Casualty of War

I was a little kid, no more than six years old, but even I knew it. The Second World War was over! No more air raids, blackouts, or sirens. Liverpool came to life again. Troopships at the Pier Head let down their gangways and men in uniform, carrying kit bags, marched ashore amid confetti and streamers. They broke ranks and charged into the crowds, to be united with their families, amid laughter, tears, and people singing, "Pack up your troubles in your old kit bag and smile!" It was a joyous time for those who had come through the war unscathed.

There were a lot of things I had never tasted, owing to food shortages and rationing, but chewing gum, real American chewing gum, was something I'd dreamed of. Everybody chewed it in the U.S. films. What did it taste like?

My pal Georgie said that American troop convoys were to come along Walton Road. We ran up there and pushed our way through the masses that thronged the pavement. I found a great spot, right at the curb edge, outside the co-op shop.

Then they came, seemingly hundreds of olive drab–painted trucks with the canvas awnings rolled back, packed with American soldiers—GIs they called them. Girls were cheering and blowing kisses to the handsome young men. We kids held our hands out and shouted, "Any gum, chum?" The soldiers tossed nylon stockings, American cigarettes, things called Tootsie Rolls, and chewing gum sticks in long foil packets.

Being only a little fellow, I didn't expect to get any. But I stuck at it. "Any gum, chum?" I roared and yelled. Suddenly, the lorries halted; I think it was for the traffic lights. I found myself looking up into a steel-helmeted soldier's smiling face. The convoy started to move away, and I shouted my plea desperately. He pulled a packet of chewing gum from his pocket and hurled it toward my outstretched hands. I was never much good at catching things. It hit me, right between my eyebrows and burst the skin. I scrabbled in the gutter, blood pouring into my left eye, and grabbed the gum. It was sweet, juicy, and sticky—all I'd imagined it to be—Juicy Fruit! I was too overjoyed to cry or worry about injuries. Darkness was falling, I dashed home and washed my face, the cut stopped bleeding, and I never stopped chewing.

Out in the street they had lit a bonfire, with a dummy Adolf Hitler sitting on top of it. The street air raid shelters had red, white, and blue victory V signs painted all over them. A gramophone was perched on a windowsill, playing "When the Lights Go On Again All over the World." Men, still in uniform, danced with wives and girlfriends. Red Cross parcels of good things to eat were being ripped open and distributed to the children.

I was with Georgie and my pals; we sat on the curb edge with our feet in the gutter. The war was over; we drank lemonade and munched real milk chocolate. Happiness was me, a kid with chocolate and pop.

Then it happened. A giant sergeant, wearing full Highland dress uniform, white spats, sporran, and kilt swirling, came waltzing past, partnering my auntie Josie. He accidentally stood right on my big toe, crushing it under his heavy boots. It was like a tram running over my foot, and I screamed in agony. Somebody picked me up and rushed into my auntie Annie's house, which was right by where I had been sitting.

It was good old Uncle Charlie, back from fighting in Italy, still in uniform with a star and ribbon on his tunic. He whipped off my shoe and sock, and sat me on the draining board in the kitchen. "Come on, lad, soldiers don't cry!" I took my clenched fists away from my eyes; I had rubbed my chewing gum cut open again. Uncle Charlie dabbed iodine on the cut, and also on my rapidly purpling toenail, while I bravely explained how both injuries had happened. He bandaged my foot, and around my brow, with a khaki silk military dressing. He also gave me an armband, then held me up to the mirror and laughed. "You've really been in the wars, haven't you, lad? Never mind, you look like a real wounded soldier now!"

I marched back out to the street party. Six years old and a real war-wounded soldier. Not bad!

Biography:
Grew up: Liverpool, England
Now lives: Liverpool, England
Random fact: Former jobs include merchant sailor, railway fireman, truck driver, folk singer, stand-up comic

Selected Bibliography:
Redwall (The Redwall series #1)
Loamhedge (The Redwall series #16)
Rakkety Tam (The Redwall series #17)

PATRICK JONES
Wrestling with Reading

You have to understand that the world was different then. I was growing up in Flint, Michigan, and was a huge fan of professional wrestling. But it wasn't like now, with just Vince and the WWE. Then, every major city had its own wrestlers: my guys were The Sheik and Bobo Brazil. Every other city had its wrestlers who would often visit Flint to fight, and lose to, The Sheik. The only way you could know about those other wrestlers was through magazines. There was no Internet, no cable, no e-mail, no way of sharing information. The only way I could find out about these other wrestlers was through the newsstand wrestling magazines.

So, I'm twelve and I go to my local public library to get something for school. I wasn't a big reader or library user; it just wasn't something I did. I'm at the library and I see a whole shelf of different magazines. As I go to check out my books, I summon up all my twelve-year-old courage and ask the librarian if the library has any wrestling magazines. That is what I thought I asked; instead I think I asked her to show me what her face would look like if she sucked on a lemon for a hundred years. She looked like she was about to stroke out at the mere mention of wrestling magazines in her library. She made me feel stupid, and I never went back.

Flash forward now to the summer of 2000. Former professional wrestler and then best-selling author Mick "Cactus Jack
Mankind Dude Love Hardcore Legend" Foley is the guest of
honor at the American Library Association convention. I'm the
one getting to ask him questions as some five hundred plus librarians sit in the audience, then later stand in line to have Foley
autograph his book. Sometimes there is justice in the universe.

So it was newsstand wrestling magazines that started me reading, and, for that matter, writing. By the time I was eight, I had
already published some articles in a wrestling fan newsletter (*In
This Corner*, edited by Danny Shelburg). After I went to college,
then graduate school, I started working in libraries. One of the
first articles I ever published was called "Wrestling with
Magazines for Teenagers," which called for libraries to buy more
magazines generally for teens, and wrestling magazines specifically. The fact that people needed to be urged to buy interesting
magazines for teens gives you an idea of how well most libraries
did in serving boys. You have to understand that the world was
different then.

Imagine my delight as the past couple of years have seen an
explosion of books written by (and sometimes for) professional
wrestlers: some about the new breed (The Rock), some about the
old legends (Freddie Blassie), and some about the best of both
worlds (Mick Foley). I don't read much fiction anymore, even
though I try to write it now. I don't read the newsstand wrestling
magazines anymore, either. Instead the highlight of every
Saturday is when the *Wrestling Observer* newsletter arrives in my
mailbox.

But maybe you don't like wrestling. That's OK, but that's not
the point. The point is how something I saw on TV captured me
and how reading everything that I could about it made me enjoy
it even more. In doing so, it made me enjoy reading, as I learned

the lesson about the value of reading for fun and for facts. Reading can be, for many folks, good in and of itself. But for me—for lots of men and boys—reading is the means to reach an end. The end being a fuller understanding, appreciation, and even expertise in an area: wrestling, baseball, fly fishing, computer graphics, model rockets, science fiction films, rap music, or martial arts. Boys want to read about something. We'll see a movie or something on TV, and want to know more. A lot more, and that is what reading books and magazines—and Web pages—can do for us.

I'm not sure what happened to that librarian in Flint, and I never got my wrestling magazines from the library. My hope is that boys going into libraries now can find wrestling magazines or something similar. Everyone has to understand that the world is different now.

Biography:

Grew up: Flint, Michigan

Now lives: Minneapolis, Minnesota

Random fact: Supported Michael Moore way back when, in his underground high school newspaper

Selected Bibliography:

Things Change
Connecting Young Adults and Libraries
What's So Scary About R. L. Stine?

DAV PILKEY

I first started drawing the Water Man comics in 1977, when I was eleven years old. My parents actually encouraged me to make these comics. They weren't too fond of my Captain Underpants and Diaper Man comics, and were trying to persuade me to make comics that were a little less "potty oriented."

So I began in November of 1977, and over the next few months compiled twenty issues of my Water Man Epic Saga. These comics featured not only Water Man and his crime-fighting pals Molecule Man and Mr. Shape-O, but also a cast of famous bad guys, including King Kong, the Invisible Man, and Jaws 2.

I started each comic by grabbing a big stack of paper. My dad always brought home paper from work for me to draw on (you might see the Republic Steel logo bleeding through some of the pages). I went through the paper as fast as my dad could bring it home.

I made my comics up as I went along. I started with the title, then made up the stories as I drew the pictures (much the same way I do today). Sometimes it worked out great . . . other times it didn't. For example, in the comic "We Must Destroy Water Man," there's only one bad guy. Who's the *we*? I didn't know

A Water Man comic by Dav Pilkey, age eleven

then, and I don't know now. Often these comics contain mis-
spelled words, and sometimes you can tell where my pen started
running out of ink as the pages piled up. But that didn't stop me.
I was on a roll.

While none of these comics are masterpieces, they always
remind me of the homemade comics that children now send me

every day. They have the same spirit. There's something about the work of a kid who is being creative on his or her own time. Nobody forces a kid to make a comic book. Kids just do it sometimes. And there is always something wonderful about that kind of spontaneous creativity. It's magic!

I'm really grateful that my parents encouraged me to make these comics, and even more grateful that they refused to let me bring them to school. I begged and pleaded, but they always said no. All of my other comics (including the ones I made in junior high and high school) have disappeared. Some were torn up by angry teachers, others were borrowed by friends who never returned them, and some just got lost. But because my parents had forbidden me to take these comics to school, I still have every single one of them. They're the only childhood comics I have left. Don't you hate it when your parents are right?

Biography:
Grew up: Cleveland, Ohio
Now lives: On an island in Washington State
Random fact: Still holds the first-grade classroom record for number of crayons stuck up a nose

Selected Bibliography
Captain Underpants series
Dogzilla
Read all of Dav's Water Man comics on his Web site at www.Pilkey.com

STEPHEN KING

from On Writing

There was a stream of babysitters during our Wisconsin period. I don't know if they left because David and I were a handful, or because they found better-paying jobs, or because my mother insisted on higher standards than they were willing to rise to; all I know is that there were a lot of them. The only one I remember with any clarity is Eula, or maybe she was Beulah. She was a teenager, she was as big as a house, and she laughed a lot. Eula-Beulah had a wonderful sense of humor, even at four I could recognize that, but it was a *dangerous* sense of humor—there seemed to be a potential thunderclap hidden inside each hand-patting, butt-rocking, head-tossing outburst of glee. When I see those hidden-camera sequences where real-life babysitters and nannies just all of a sudden wind up and clout the kids, it's my days with Eula-Beulah I always think of.

Was she as hard on my brother David as she was on me? I don't know. He's not in any of these pictures. Besides, he would have been less at risk from Hurricane Eula-Beulah's dangerous winds; at six, he would have been in the first grade and off the gunnery range for most of the day.

Eula-Beulah would be on the phone, laughing with someone, and beckon me over. She would hug me, tickle me, get me laughing, and then, still laughing, go upside my head hard enough to knock me down. Then she would tickle me with her bare feet until we were both laughing again.

Eula-Beulah was prone to farts—the kind that are both loud and smelly. Sometimes when she was so afflicted, she would throw me on the couch, drop her wool-skirted butt on my face, and let loose. "Pow!" she'd cry in high glee. It was like being buried in marsh-gas fireworks. I remember the dark, the sense that I was suffocating, and I remember laughing. Because, while what was happening was sort of horrible, it was also sort of funny. In many ways, Eula-Beulah prepared me for literary criticism. After having a two-hundred-pound babysitter fart on your face and yell Pow! *The Village Voice* holds few terrors.

Biography:

Grew up: Portland, Maine, then Fort Wayne, Indiana, then Durham, Maine

Now lives: Florida, and Bangor and Center Lovell, Maine

Random facts: Met his wife in a library; sometimes uses pen name Richard Bachman

Selected Bibliography:

Pet Sematary
On Writing
The Dark Tower books

DAVID KLASS
Pop

I remember how embarrassed I was when Pop announced that he was going to join my summer league team as an assistant coach. He was a college professor. Plump. A gray beard. Not particularly athletic. "But you don't know anything about baseball."

"I know lots about baseball," he assured me. "I've been a Mets fan for years."

"Yeah, but you don't know how to play baseball. You can't even throw."

That stopped him for a second. That hurt. "It'll be OK," he said. "Trust me."

I remember him at practice, devising a way to chart balls and strikes for the pitchers. Other dads hitting fungos, throwing for batting practice, demonstrating technique. Mine with a pen and a pad, explaining his new method. How ashamed I felt.

Other dads driving us to away games. One of them sipping whiskey from a brown paper bag as he steered. Another cocking his finger each time we passed someone who wasn't Caucasian. Black, Asian, Hispanic, didn't matter. "Bang," he'd say. "Got another."

Kids in the car would laugh. *How daring*, I thought.

Pop driving us to an away game. We pass two guys walking

side by side. A kid on my team rolls down the window. "Homos," he shouts. My dad pulls the car over to the curb. "Just for your information," he says, "*homo-* is a Greek root. It means 'equal' or 'like.' As in *homogeneous*. It also means 'man,' from the Latin. As in *Homo sapiens*. So if you were trying to say those two guys are alike, or that they're both men, you were right. Otherwise you don't know what you're talking about."

He drives on. Kids in the car look at me. Your dad is weird.

Away soccer games in high school. Pop shows up at every single one. Stands on grass, watching and unconsciously kicking his feet. "Looks like your dad wants to play," a teammate snickers.

One game in South Jersey. Bus ride takes more than an hour. Driver gets lost. We go over a bridge, down back roads, through marsh. Finally find soccer field. Pop is waiting there, all alone. He waves.

"You know, you don't have to come to every single game," I finally tell him.

"I know," he says.

It's only later, in college, that I start to fully appreciate what a wise, gentle, wonderful father I have.

Now, at forty-three, I still play in soccer games. Pop isn't there anymore. How badly I miss him. How very lucky I was.

Biography:
Grew up: Leonia, New Jersey
Now lives: New York City
Random fact: Mom, dad, and both sisters are writers, too

Selected Bibliography
California Blue
You Don't Know Me
Danger Zone

GORDON KORMAN
Guy Things

Like many guys my age, I grew up on Looney Tunes. As a kid, I was a total addict, but over the years, I've lost touch with those old classic cartoons.

The other day, I happened to catch the one about the voyage of Christopher Columbus.

Columbus was with the king of Spain, explaining his theory of the shape of the earth. "It is round," he declared, "like your head!"

I was already laughing. I remembered this one. The king was going to counter, "It is flat"—and then wallop the explorer-to-be with an enormous mallet, pancaking his cranium—"like your head!"

It didn't happen. Instead, the story continued with Columbus being ejected from the palace, and went on to his secret meeting with the queen. I was thunderstruck. Someone had cut out the best part of the cartoon!

Okay, Looney Tunes are pretty old stuff. It makes sense that they've been edited over the years. But why does it always have to be the guy parts that end up on the chopping block? "It is flat"—*wham!*—"like your head!" That's a guy scene if there ever was one. True, many girls probably get a kick out of it, too. But with guys, there's more to it than that. For us, the contents of the world are divided into guy things and non-guy things. And the distinction is as clear-cut as up versus down, hot versus cold, night versus day. It's instinct. We're born with it.

The following things are, without question, one-hundred-percent non-guy: good smells, princesses, salad, figure skating, cuteness, bedtime, yoga, all fat-free products (except nitroglycerine), periwinkle blue, periwinkles, and three-quarters of the books your librarian describes as award-winners.

Compare this to the core list of guy things: bad smells, Cartoon Network, jock itch, torque, XGames, X-rays, XBox, underwater explosions, Monty Python, gas (all varieties), professional wrestling (including sumo), and any injury that involves something being hyperextended.

Naturally, none of this is carved in stone. Flowers, for example, can be guy things, provided they're lethally poisonous. Or if they've been genetically altered to fire bursts of bioengineered spores that will allow evil scientists to take control of unsuspecting innocent minds.

It works the other way, too. On the surface, dinosaurs are the ultimate guy things. What could be cooler than a T. rex—a twenty-foot-tall killing machine armed with crushing jaws of six-inch razor-sharp knives? But when you turn on the TV, the dino you see there is purple, with no teeth and a butt like an over-stuffed beanbag chair. And he's singing a song about looking both ways before you cross the street.

That Mesozoic mama's boy wouldn't have lasted five seconds in the Cretaceous period.

It's tough to be a guy. Half the time, we're not allowed to be ourselves. And even when we are, we're sort of expected to apologize for it, as if enjoying a good Tyrannosaur rampage is shameful or something.

Well, at least we've got sports. That's our dominion. Slam-dunk-checkered-flag-Super-Bowl-out-of-the-park-he-shoots-he-scores—no non-guy things in there, right?

I was born and raised in Canada, so our big sport was hockey. I'll never forget the first year I played on a real team. We had all the big kids—we were definitely going to be the intimidators of the league. It was our destiny.

Then we got our uniforms, fresh from the sponsor. Our coach ripped open the box and held up the first jersey:

PRETTY POLLY PAINT AND WALLPAPER

FALCONS

The only sound in the locker room was my jaw hitting the cement floor. Oh, yeah—people were really going to be scared of us. They would quake in their skates at the prospect of facing off against Pretty Polly.

How could such absolute non-guyness have wormed its way into this sacred inner sanctum of guy-hood?

We might as well have been sponsored by the Pampers Corporation. I don't care how tough you are; the Diaper Squad intimidates nobody.

I just heard that they now have a peewee league that doesn't keep score. Can you believe that? Doesn't keep score! If you don't keep score, how do you know who wins?

Duh!

Winning—that's another guy thing. And losing, too. What could be more glorious, more heroic than giving it your best shot and going down in flames?

Sure, we may pitch a fit, blame the refs, turn the air blue with our ranting. But we can handle it. We realize it's only a game, just like we understand that braining someone with an oversized mallet is not an appropriate response to a disagreement about the shape of the planet.

We know it as well as we know the topography of the rinks and courts and fields where we play our beloved sports.

They're flat—*wham!*—like our heads.

Biography:

Grew up: Toronto, Canada

Now lives: Long Island, New York

Random fact: At age two, wanted to be a dog when he grew up, and used to eat dinner under the table

Selected Bibliography:

No More Dead Dogs

The Climb (Everest series #2)

The Deep (Dive series #2)

JERRY PINKNEY
Role-Playing and Discovery

NAT LOVE

On Saturdays, after household chores were finished, I would meet up with my best friends. Off we would rush to the movies. Tickets were ten cents, and there was always a double feature. I was most excited when there were westerns. As a young boy growing up in Philadelphia, Pennsylvania, I dreamed of exploring the early frontier.

BILL PICKETT

JP

My friends and I played at being cowboys and explorers. With much enthusiasm and intensity, we inhabited the characters portrayed on the silver screen. We fashioned our costumes and gear from what we could find at home or purchase from the local five-and-dime store. I would whittle out of wood a bowie knife modeled after the one Jim Bowie had at his side while defending the Alamo. I would then take my turn at being Roy Rogers, the cowboy, or Daniel Boone, the famous pioneer, journeying through the rugged wilderness.

If anyone had asked at that time if my excitement was due to an early interest in history, my answer would have been a resounding, "No!" However, looking back, I realize that answer would not have been entirely true. Yes, we did have fun, and yes, our flights into the past seemed to be more about action than about learning history, but that role-playing seeded my interest in discovery. When I learned as an adult that one out of three cowboys was black or Mexican, that discovery was moving and profound.

I do wonder, though, how we would have been affected as young boys if, at that impressionable time, we had known about Nat Love, a cowboy; Bill Pickett, a rodeo cowboy; Jim Beckwourth, a fur trader; or Jean Baptiste Du Sable, the explorer—all persons of African descent.

Biography:
Grew up: Philadelphia, Pennsylvania
Now lives: Croton-on-Hudson, New York
Random fact: Even wearing a coonskin cap, couldn't get anyone to believe he was Daniel Boone

Selected Bibliography:
Black Cowboy, Wild Horses: A True Story by Julius Lester
Uncle Remus: The Complete Tales by Julius Lester
John Henry by Julius Lester

ERIK P. KRAFT

Busted

You know what I hate about the bus?

Well, I guess a few things.

The smell, the filthy guy yelling, "I'm a homeowner now!" (I hope this home has a shower, sir.)

These things are up there, but I can kind of deal with them because the bus doesn't *always* smell (just frequently), and I imagine Mr. Homeowner will be involved in various fix-it-up projects after today. But it really bugs me when I can only see the back of the head of what could possibly be a very cute girl. I mean, I've seen some pretty cute backs of heads on this bus, but how am I supposed to be sure she's cute from five rows back? Sometimes you can catch a profile if she turns to look out the window or something, but profiles can lie. You need to see someone straight-on to be absolutely sure. Unless you sit at the front and stare back at everyone, you're not going to have the right angle. And if you do that, well, it's kind of creepy.

I wish there were stricter rules about who could buy little barrettes and tiny powder-blue T-shirts. That could go a long way toward easing my mind, but I guess the ability to buy any clothing and accessories you want is what makes our country great.

I suppose I could just walk up, take a good look, and then go sit back down, but then I'd feel like I was only a few steps away from being the next Mr. Homeowner. Usually the best I can do is sneak a quick glance as I get off at my stop, but not too long. I'd really hate to blow it with a girl I'm never going to see again.

Yeah, I hate the bus.

Biography:

Grew up: East Longmeadow, Massachusetts
Now lives: Boston, Massachusetts
Random fact: Has a cat named Phil who likes bologna

Selected Bibliography:

Lenny and Mel
Lenny and Mel's Summer Vacation
Lenny and Mel After-School Confidential

DAVID LUBAR

Copies

At least I had company this year. I hate getting dragged to Dad's office for Kids Come to Work Day. It's so boring, I want to scream. But my little brother was finally old enough to come.

"You kids are in for a treat," Dad said when we pulled into the parking lot. "We got a new shredder for the office. Bet you can't wait to see that baby in action, right?"

"Right, Dad," I said, grabbing hold of Nicky by the collar so he wouldn't wander into the path of any of the dozens of cars zipping through the parking lot.

Dad kept describing the wonders that lay ahead of us. "And we just put in two new copiers."

Shoot. When he said that, I realized I'd forgotten to bring anything to copy. It's fun to run off a couple hundred copies of a cartoon and pass them out at school. But I didn't have anything with me. Wait. That wasn't true. I had Nicky. The moment we got inside, I asked if I could go to the copy room.

"Sure," Dad said. "You know the way. Just don't fool around too much. The company has a policy against personal copies."

"Hey, don't worry," I said. "Come on, Nicky, I'll show you Dad's spiffy new copiers." I grinned at the thought of how personal a copy could be.

I led Nicky down the hall to the copy room. We were in luck. The place was all ours. "Here," I said, pulling a chair over to the copier. "Get up."

Nicky hopped onto the chair. I lifted the lid of the copier. "Put your face on the glass," I said. "But close your eyes. It can get real bright."

Nicky did what I said. I set the machine for ten copies, but my finger slipped. It showed 1,000. *Hey, why not?* I thought, deciding to leave the number the way it was.

"Here goes," I said, hitting the COPY button.

Man, it was fast. Copies started coming out like bullets from a machine gun. They looked real cool. Nicky had his face scrunched up, but you could tell it was him.

I glanced at the other copier and got another idea. I almost didn't do it, but I couldn't resist. Hey—what's the harm? I slipped down my pants and sat on the machine. I'd heard about kids doing this, but I'd never tried it. I reached over and hit the buttons. Might as well make a thousand copies of my butt, to go along with the thousand of Nicky's face. Talk about a perfect pair.

My machine was even faster. Before I knew it, I'd run off the thousand copies. I hopped down and went back over to Nicky.

"Hey, these aren't any good," I said, grabbing a copy as it shot out of the machine. The image was faded. I thumbed through the stack. Maybe the machine was running out of supplies. Each copy that came out was a bit more faded.

"Can I get up now?" Nicky asked as the machine hummed to a stop. His voice sounded really muffled.

"Sure. Yeah. It's done."

Nicky stood up.

For a moment, I just stared. Then I blinked.

That was more than Nicky could do. His nose and mouth and eyelids were gone. Almost everything was gone. It had been copied away. Two small holes were all that was left of his nose. A pair of eyes stared out at me from a face like an egg.

Oh man, Dad was going to kick my butt.

My butt!

I raced to the other machine and looked at the last copy that came out. Nothing. Just a smooth, round hunk of flesh.

When my hand stopped shaking, I reached down the back of my pants. Smoothness. No crack. Nothing.

Nicky made some kind of noise in his throat, but I couldn't understand it. Without a mouth, he couldn't talk.

It was about then that I realized something awful. It was bad enough that Nicky couldn't talk. But I had to go to the bathroom. And without a butt, I couldn't do that, either.

Biography:

Grew up: Morristown, New Jersey

Plans to die: Mars

Random fact: Once played the bottom half of a giraffe (theatrically, not musically)

Selected Bibliography:

Dunk

Hidden Talents

In the Land of the Lawn Weenies and Other Misadventures

VLADIMIR RADUNSKY
When All Bicycles Were Black

The most vivid memories of my childhood, I realize now, are connected with bicycles.

I was born in Russia fifty years ago. And I grew up there. For many, especially in the countryside and in small towns, a bicycle was the means of transportation. It is hard to imagine now, but in those times (soon after World War II), a bicycle in Russia was almost an impossible luxury. The country was poor and bicycles were few and hard to get.

They even looked different back then. They were painted a shiny black, and the saddle was made of real leather with gleaming steel shock absorbers underneath. The women's bicycles were different from the men's: the frame was made so that it was easy to get on even in a dress. (Women rarely wore pants in those days.)

Most children could only dream about having a bike of their own: a "Scholastic" for the littlest ones, an "Eagle" for the older set. They cost a lot and children grow quickly, so parents preferred to wait until a child was ready for a grown-up bike.

Yet children wanted to ride so badly that they were ready to get on any available bicycle, even those almost twice their size. They rode standing up, threading one leg under the bar in order to reach the pedal, and raising their hands way above their heads to grab the handlebar. A bunch of smaller children would run behind the happy owner, trying to get their turn.

I learned to ride by myself when I was about seven. This is how it happened.

I did not have a bicycle of my own. But a neighbor boy's father got himself a bicycle. The bicycle was huge of course, and of course it was black. I was struck by its beauty. Even just touching it—its tires, its saddle—was a pleasure.

We took the bicycle by the handlebar and walked it around and around the courtyard, not sure how to begin. But even doing that was a fascinating game. The boy's father looked out the window and laughed. "This is one lucky bike, having all the fun!"

Then my partner got bored and I got the bicycle all to myself and walked it around and around until it was dusk and my parents called me home.

The next morning, when I came outside, there was no one around. The black beauty was leaning against the wall, waiting for me. Its shadow on the wall was even prettier than the bike itself.

I made up my mind: I threaded my right leg under the bar, reached the pedal (as I had seen the other children do so many times), raised my hands way above my head and grabbed the handlebars, and . . . took off! I can't explain how it happened, but I just took off.

And since then, one of my greatest pleasures in life is just to get on my bike and take off. Doesn't matter where.

Biography:

Grew up: Moscow, Russia

Now lives: New York, New York, and Rome, Italy

Random fact: When daydreaming while riding, once rode his bicycle into a ditch

Selected Bibliography:

Yucka Drucka Droni

Ten

The Maestro Plays by Bill Martin Jr.

CHRIS LYNCH

The Pellet in the Paint Can

"You have the most superb ACNE."

My dad, as one of the country's top Internet psychologists, has to be quotable. Specifically, he is in the business of giving people advice through his Web site and subscription newsletter on the psychology of the family, and even more specifically on the psychology of the *blended* family, which we ourselves happen to be. So he is an expert. And he has to be quotable. If you don't whip up new terms and catchphrases and case studies all the time in the online psychology business, you become yesterday's news today.

"Haven't I always said you have the best ACNE of any of us?"

That would be A.C.N.E.: Adult-Child Nonbiological Engagement. It means I get along with my stepmother. I'd have to have some pretty rancid ACNE *not* to get along with her, since Beverly is easy to know and deep-fries everything she cooks and has some very nice legs, though you didn't hear that from me.

"I mean, I like to think I have some fairly strong ACNE with the girls, but even we can't match you and Beverly."

Right, the girls. They are twins. Bad enough you have to blend, right, but then you're expected to blend with two people who are the exact same person. How's a guy supposed to crack that? There is no actual way of telling them apart if they don't want you to, and that drives me right out of my tree, and they know it drives me right out of my tree, and out of my tree is where they want me.

The only single consistent difference is the smell. One of them usually smells like Glow, by Jennifer Lopez, and the other one smells like Still, by Jennifer Lopez. Glow is really *last* year's J. Lo, so there's a bit of contention there, which is nice.

So one day I am hanging around after school and one of them comes into my room. My room. *One* of them. I had never seen just one of them before. Not such a mind-bending experience, you say? Well mine was bent right over. I just couldn't cope with the sight of one of them alone. To me it was like having a person with maybe half a head walk into the room scooping out brains and asking if I wanted some.

"Who are you?" I asked. She giggled. But of course. As my discomfort increased, so did the giggling. There was an untwinned twin in front of me, and she was perfume-free. Couldn't tell if I had Glow here or Still. "Where is the other one?" I demanded. I was going right out of my tree, flustered and paranoid over the fact that I did not know which one I had here, as if it would make *any* difference, as if I would even *care* who was who if they were both here, but there you go. Right out of my tree.

Until the giggling—in my own room, remember—got just unbearable, horrifying, like a thousand giggling twins, no, an odd number, 999 giggling twins were in my room and I didn't know any of them from the others and *why* do twins find that so funny anyway, and I just had to do something.

I marched right past her. She followed, giggling madly away, until I reached her room, their room. "You can't go in there," she said, not giggling anymore. I just went in. She kept saying, "Hey, hey, hey." I kept saying nothing.

I reached the dresser, reached the altar of Jennifer Lopez

where all the tubes and bottles and sprays and gunks were arranged in front of the mirror in two very distinct groupings. "Leave that alone," she said.

"I think I won't," I said. I picked up one small precious-looking bottle, whirled around, and aimed.

"Don't do it," she said, with a whole new seriousness.

I smiled. "You be Still," I said, and . . . *schpritzzz* . . .

The game was up before the front door even closed.

Her voice was like a furious seagull that could do words. "What are you doing with my Still by Jennifer Lopez?!" she screamed, running up the stairs two at a time to have a meeting with her sister to discuss the relative merits of last year's and this year's J. Lo.

It was beautiful. It was like living inside of a pro hockey game that smelled really nice. If dad hadn't come home to lay some ACNE on them, there might have been a fatality.

"Why do you do these things, son?"

"Sorry, Dad. I don't blend very well, I guess. I guess you can't write about me anymore. Where's Beverly? I'll blend with her."

I don't cope well with changes or surprises. Dad says it may be a response to the overabundance of changes and surprises in my young life. I say it may be a response to my dad being a shrinky-dink.

"What did we say happens when you refer to my job as shrinky-dink?"

"It belittles us all."

"Right, son, and we don't want that. And we don't want you disrupting the household. You do blend. We all blend. In fact, we need you more than anyone. You are like that little iron pellet inside the can of spray paint, causing the whole contents of the can to blend together smoothly, harmoniously, into one lovely color."

The two of us stood there for a minute, staring at each other.
"I am that little iron pellet?" I said.

"Yes, son, you are that little iron pellet. But think about it. Without the other contents of that can of paint, the pellet doesn't do anything so beautiful. All it does is rattle and rattle around in that can, making that god-awful racket that drives everyone to distraction. . . ."

As he finished, his voice trailed off, his head tilted sideways, and I could see him composing a newsletter piece in his head. He patted my cheek and ran toward his study, mouthing the words *paint* and *pellet*.

I rolled it around in my head. The pellet in the paint can. Of course. That god-awful racket that drives everyone to distraction.

"I *love* that sound."

Biography:

Grew up: Boston, Massachusetts
Now lives: Scotland
Random fact: Has Homer Simpson slippers

Selected Bibliography:

Slot Machine
Extreme Elvin
Iceman

JOHN MARSDEN
Unfinished Business

Here's the story. I'm in a shop, trying on a pair of jeans. I go into the little cubicle, pull the curtain shut, take off my trousers, and start pulling on the jeans.

Suddenly the curtain is pulled open. I look up, startled. A young guy, maybe nineteen or twenty, is standing there. He's a lot younger, taller, and stronger and bigger than I am. He says, "I left eighty bucks in here. Where's my eighty bucks?"

I try to stay calm, and I answer, "Sorry, I can't help you. There wasn't any money here."

The young saleswoman comes along. She's only about seventeen or eighteen, and lightly built. She pulls at him, saying, "You can't do that. You can't walk in on people like that."

He turns away, saying, "But I left my money in there. He's got my money." I pull the curtain shut and continue to try on the jeans, still trying to be calm.

The jeans fit pretty well. I start taking them off. The curtain gets ripped open again. Of course it's the same guy. Now he's really boiling. "Where's my money, man? I want my money. Give me my eighty bucks."

I'm quite proud of the fact that I don't look weak and I don't start trembling.

"I've told you, there's no money in here. You must have left it somewhere else." But he won't listen. I'll leave the swear words out from what he said, which will make this story about twenty percent shorter, but he keeps standing there demanding his money, getting angrier and angrier.

Once again the girl comes and pulls him away. I admire her strength. I hear him complaining to a friend about how I've stolen his money and how he's going to get it off me.

I come out of the cubicle and take the jeans to the counter. I'm nervous enough to think about abandoning the shopping trip and walking out of the shop, but I'm determined not to be frightened and not to look frightened. This guy and his friend are near the counter, the guy swearing continuously at me and demanding his money, his friend listening sympathetically, but not getting involved.

I pull out my wallet to pay for the jeans. The guy walks toward me, saying, "You've got my eighty bucks. I want to look in your wallet."

"Back off," I tell him. "Just back off."

He does, rather to my surprise. I'm relieved to know that there's a line he still won't cross.

The jeans are fifty dollars, but I'm so disturbed that I give the salesgirl eighty dollars.

She says, "They're only fifty." I quickly stuff the other thirty dollars back in my wallet. Luckily the guy doesn't seem to have noticed.

I get my jeans in a bag, along with a sympathetic smile from the sales assistant. The young man continues to stare at me and abuse me, saying to his friend, "I know he's got it. If I could just prove that he has it . . ."

I head out of the shop. I don't want to run straight to my car. I want to show this guy that he hasn't gotten to me. Of course the truth is that I did steal his eighty bucks. . . . Nuh, just kidding. Just checking that you're awake. Anyway, after a few minutes I do walk out to the car. I get in, start the engine, and pull out from the curb. But all the time I'm thinking, *I don't want to go; this is unfinished business.*

I drive toward the intersection, really troubled about leaving the situation. Something tells me that I have to resolve this. I do a U-turn, still not sure what to do, and then I see the two young guys walking along the footpath, not far from my car. I pull over next to them, jump out of the car and call to them. They look startled.

By now I do know what I want to do. I say to the tall one, the angry one, "I want to show you something about human beings. I want to prove something to you."

I get out my wallet again and open it. I realize they are too close for comfort. I put up one hand and say, "Back up, both of you."

They do, and again I think, *Good, they're still not totally out of control.*

I've decided that I will give the guy $160. If I give him eighty he'll think I did steal his money and he's scared me into returning it. But I'm too nervous to stand there counting out $160. So I take two hundreds and push them at him. "Here's two hundred bucks," I say. "And the next time you start judging people, the next time you're so certain you're right, just remember that maybe you're actually wrong."

Their whole attitude changes. These guys are of Middle Eastern appearance, and the quieter one suddenly starts showering me with Islamic blessings, blessing me, my family, my home, my car . . . The taller one tilts his head. He seems disconcerted, but kind of admiring, and he finally says, "You're a madman, but yes, bless you."

They walk on laughing and talking to each other and still shaking their heads. I go back to the car, do another U-turn. By the time I get through the intersection, they're halfway down the next block. I turn left, and they see me. They wave affectionately, enthusiastically.

I go home.

It would be nice if the story ended there, and I could make a few smart comments about how I'd changed the life of this aggressive young man. But about a week later I was in the same shopping center, going past the same shop, and I caught the eye of the young saleswoman. She clearly remembered me, and smiled and waved. I went in. She was full of talk about the incident. She told me that after I had left the shop, the guy had found his money, which he'd put in his watch pocket instead of his regular pocket. When he came back the next day and told her how I'd given him two hundred bucks, she was furious with him. "I told him that he was a complete shit," she said. "I told him, 'How could you take that man's money? Don't you have any morals at all? You're disgusting.' He just said that you were this stupid guy with stacks of money, and so he didn't care."

Well, I still think I got good value for my two hundred dollars. I spent that money to jolt him, to shock him. He'll remember it for the rest of his life. He will never be quite certain about people again. No matter what he said to the sales assistant, I believe he was shaken, because he came face-to-face with something he couldn't fit into his understanding of the world.

I think he sees the world as a place where everyone is after all that they can get, where everyone's trying to rip everyone else off. Now, he can't be quite so sure.

I think there are a lot of men who are more like children than men. Men who sulk, who throw tantrums when they don't get what they want, who complain that their workmates or their boss or their parents or their customers or their government are against them, men who want a golden goose to lay golden eggs in their backyard while they sit inside watching TV, men who make racist or sexist jokes, men who resent everybody who's got more money than they have and despise everybody who's got less money than they have.

It's really hard for a boy to become a man, and in our society not many boys do. The challenge for a boy is to become a man who has integrity, strength, kindness, and understanding. How many men do you know who are like that? I don't know many.

I am not a brave or strong person. When I went to school, rugby was compulsory for all the boys, and the teams were graded by ability, from A through H. So, for example, the best fifteen-year-old players were in the Under-16 As, and the worst were in the Under-16 Hs.

For the whole of my school career, I was reserve for the Hs.

But the other day, in that jeans shop, I was strong.

Biography:

Grew up: Melbourne, Australia, and Devonport, Tasmania
Now lives: Melbourne, Australia
Random fact: Dislikes lumpy custard, most reviewers, and high school math courses

Selected Bibliography:

Tomorrow, When the War Began (Book One of the Tomorrow series)

The Dead of Night (Book Two of the Tomorrow series)

A Killing Frost (Book Three of the Tomorrow series)

SERGIO RUZZIER

I've always liked to draw monsters. Here's a recent one from Karla Kuskin's collection of poems *Moon, Have You Met My Mother?*

But the one that is dearest to me is the Sprokostagorubolonoso, the main character of a comic book I wrote and illustrated as a school assignment in fourth grade. It was actually supposed to be an essay written in Italian, but my teacher, Mrs. Santarelli, was very understanding and gave me a lot of freedom, which I believe is always the best way to encourage someone to be creative.

"*Bu!*" is Italian for "Boo!"

Biography:

Grew up: Milan, Italy

Now lives: Brooklyn, New York

Random fact: One of his favorite games was "Who Dies Better?"—a kid pretended to shoot his gun at the other kids, who had to perform spectacular deaths. The best one would take the place of the shooter.

Selected Bibliography:

Why Mole Shouted and Other Stories by Lore Segal
The Little Giant
Moon, Have You Met My Mother? by Karla Kuskin

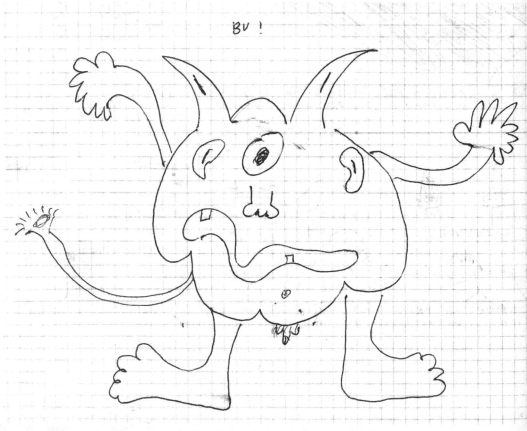

WALTER DEAN MYERS
Daydreams

So, there I was, ten years old and thinking how I would love to beat up Jerry Hart. I knew I couldn't beat up Jerry Hart, because we had already fought three times and I had lost three times. I was also afraid of his sister, Ruby, who had only beaten me up once. True life was miserable but my daydreams were flat-out wonderful. In my daydreams I could see Jerry crouching in fear as I stood over him, fists balled, a determined look on my face, while he trembled and blew snot bubbles. Yeah.

By the time I was eleven, basketball had entered my life. I knew I was going to be a star and I could dream about myself playing in the NBA. My strength was my outside shot and in my dreams I always made the last, desperate shot that swished through the net just as the buzzer sounded.

When I was thirteen, Dreanna Winfield entered my life, and my dreams. Dreanna had brushed against me in social studies and I had sort of touched her . . . err . . . chest. Yes, girls were different from boys. My daydreams became a lot more complicated. Basketball games now had cheerleaders (who all looked like Dreanna) and some very serious touching.

At fifteen I was deep into girls and basketball. Okay, so maybe I was deep into basketball and wished I was deep into girls.

Sixteen was wonderful. Almost all of my daydreams dealt with S-E-X. I still hadn't figured out exactly how the parts fit but my best friend, Eric, had told me not to worry, that girls were eager to show me. Eric and I had learned to daydream together.

I was into writing and poetry at sixteen and read a lot of English war poems. Now my daydreams shifted freely between sex, basketball, and war, with some interesting combinations. I am lying in an austere hospital somewhere in the Pacific; the nurse who comes into my room looks at me in pity and admiration. She reached for the buttons on her blouse and . . .

I joined the army on my seventeenth birthday. In the army daydreams were interrupted by the reality of fear. The army is not a good place for daydreaming.

At twenty I was a veteran and bogged down in a real factory job. I also began to write down my daydreams. I created characters to fulfill them and plots to organize their adventures. When some of the daydreams/stories sold to magazines, I began to think of myself as the Famous Writer. Girls would throw themselves at my feet! I would do a story about basketball and the Knicks would be so impressed they would ask me to join the team! Ex-nuns would fall in love with me! Life would be wonderful!

By the age of thirty, I pretty much knew what S-E-X was about and where all the good parts were located. I also knew about revisions. What I had learned to do was to dream my dreams, and then revise them if they didn't work out the way I wanted. So if the girl in the first dream (the one to whom I had dedicated the winning shot) still didn't love me, I could add my heroic donation of life-saving blood to her desperately ill and slightly slutty twin.

My dad, a janitor all of his life, once asked me what I did for a living, since he had noticed that I didn't go out to work. I gave him a long story about characterization, plot, outlining, etc. I just didn't feel right saying that all I did was write down my day-dreams.

Biography:

Grew up: The raucous streets of Harlem, New York

Now lives: Jersey City, New Jersey

Random fact: Has always had just a *little bit* of trouble separating his dreams from what he has heard is REAL LIFE

Selected Bibliography:

Bad Boy: A Memoir

Monster

Handbook for Boys

GARTH NIX
Lucky Dave

Twenty years ago I saw a guy jump out of a moving helicopter. I was sitting next to him at the time. We were about thirty feet up and doing maybe twenty miles per hour as the Huey headed in to land. Lucky Dave (as I'll call him) was next to the open door, and I was looking out past him. Then there was suddenly no one between me and the door.

The crew chief behind me swore and said something on his intercom and we suddenly plummeted down a hundred yards short of the planned landing zone. Within seconds, we were all out and running across the bush clearing toward Dave's body.

He was lying on his back, not moving. His greens looked completely black, apparently sodden with blood. His rifle was nearby, the stock and pistol grip broken off.

As we sprinted toward him, Dave suddenly stood up. We stopped in disbelief and he shouted, "Who tapped my shoulder?"

He wasn't sodden with blood. The two plastic water bottles in his pack and the two bottles in his webbing had exploded as he hit the ground, soaking him. Maybe they took some of the impact. Dave was not only alive, he wasn't even badly hurt.

It turned out that Dave had kept his eyes screwed shut in the helicopter because he was afraid of heights. He knew the crew chief would tap him on the shoulder when we landed, to tell him to get out. But his own rifle had shifted and the barrel hit him. So he jumped.

That's how he first became Lucky Dave. In the five years we served together as part-time soldiers in the Australian Army Reserve, Lucky Dave managed to do numerous unfortunate things, including:

• jump out of a moving helicopter,

• start the outboard motor of an assault boat on full throttle and fall overboard, and

• drive a truck with a jammed accelerator and faulty brakes through a town.

I guess I was lucky, too, because I was in the assault boat when Dave stood up at the stern and yanked the starter cord, and I was in the back of that speeding truck with the rest of the platoon, sound asleep until the suddenly bumpy ride alerted us to the fact that Lucky Dave was at it again.

Dave was just one of many unusual characters in our Assault Pioneer platoon, one of the inhabitants of the strange world that from 1980 to 1985 I entered for one weekend every month and for one or two months every year.

You'd think that no one would want to serve with Lucky Dave. But he was a good guy, always ready to work hard, and he *was* lucky. Despite his misfortunes, he never got himself or anyone else badly hurt or in permanent trouble.

One of the things I learned back then, and have found to be generally true since, is that it's what you do that counts, not what you say. Whether we were out on the demolition range, on a ten-day evasion exercise in a remote rainforest, or chainsawing trees to clear a landing zone, the "real men" weren't the loud-mouthed, super gung-ho guys. Those types were always the first to freak out at some unexploded ordnance or faint from heat exhaustion or drop a tree on someone because they hadn't paid attention in training.

The "real men" were the quiet, thoughtful guys who knew what to do and did it, the little wiry guys who kept going and going despite everything, and the guys like Lucky Dave. A man who could fall out of a helicopter, but still be back with his platoon two days later, black and blue all over—but laughing at his own mistake.

Biography:

Grew up: Canberra, Australia

Now lives: Sydney, Australia

Random fact: Has one yellow eye and one blue eye. Also doesn't tell the truth. About the color of his eyes, among other things. But then he usually admits when he isn't telling the truth.

Selected Bibliography:

The Abhorsen Trilogy

The Fall (The Seventh Tower series #1)

Castle (The Seventh Tower series #2)

KENNETH OPPEL
Anything Can Happen

I'd never have agreed to it, if I'd had anything better to do. It was Friday night, and I made sure to arrive good and late, so everyone would think it had been a real struggle for me to get here. Brady answered the door.

"All right! Come on in, everyone's here."

I followed him downstairs to the rec room. Most of the lights were off. In the gloom, a bunch of guys were sitting around a big table, looking pretty revved up. They all had pads of graph paper and little Ziploc bags of dice and open manuals filled with charts and tables, and they were all making notes and talking about potions and hit points and magical weapons. It was a real geek-fest. I recognized them from school, but I'd never really talked to them. The only reason I hung around with Brady was because we'd been friends since we were five. Actually, he was pretty much the only kid I hung around with since, for reasons unknown to me, the cool kids hadn't yet realized how very cool I was.

"Grab a seat beside Zolganeth," Brady said to me.

"Zolganeth?"

"We don't use real names here."

"You're kidding."

"It makes the game more fun. I'm Racknor." He pointed. "That's Wolf Larson, and Van Doom."

"What about him?" I said, nodding to the guy at the end of the table, half hidden behind a wall of propped-up books.

"He doesn't have a name."

"Why not?"

"He's the Dungeon Master. He controls the game."

"What's with the wall?"

"So we can't see the maps or anything. You should pick a name for yourself."

"Biff."

"Well, um, maybe another name?"

"What's wrong with Biff?" I knew I was being a jerk. "How about Maximus?"

"Excellent name," said Van Doom.

"We set up a character for you," Brady said, "just to save some time. He's really cool. A third-level elf Mindslayer."

"Do I get a sword?"

"A big one. And you've got psionic powers, too."

"What's that?"

"You can zap things just by using your brain."

I'd never played a game like this before. There was no board, and no pieces to move around. We were adventurers, plundering an ancient tomb. The Dungeon Master described everything to us, and we had to make our own map, and tell him what we wanted to do. There was a lot of dice rolling. I liked the dice. I'd never seen dice that were eight-sided and four-sided and twenty-sided. As we played, I kept picking them up, rattling them around in my hand, feeling all the sides with my thumb.

We skulked around the tomb, looking for treasure and secret passageways. Everyone seemed to know what they were doing, and they kept trying to explain things to me, but I pretended to only half-listen, because I didn't want them to think I was too interested. The monsters were the best part. We got to fight with orcs and carrion crawlers and sometimes they'd be carrying bags of gold or magical armor or potions. After we defeated a swarm of mutant cockroaches, we found, strapped to one of their shells, a map of the tombs marked with a big "X" and a scribbled note about an unimaginable hoard of treasure: gold, silver, and glistening gems.

I was actually starting to get into it, and then Van Doom fell into a big pit. Everyone started arguing about the best way to rescue him. I just wanted to haul him out of there and find that amazing treasure room. But everyone started arguing about whether we should use up one of our levitate spells to bring Van Doom up, or if someone should just go down on a rope, and who that would be, and if there were booby traps, and who was wearing the lightest armor. And suddenly the game was no fun anymore, because it wasn't a game, but a bunch of geeks in a basement rec room. The treasure didn't seem that interesting anymore—because somewhere out there in the real world on Friday night, there were all these amazing things going on.

"I can't believe it," I said. "Everyone's hanging out at the food court and movie theaters and having a good time, and talking and laughing and looking at girls and drinking milk shakes and I'm sitting around in a basement with Van Doom and Racknor."

Everyone was staring at me like I'd escaped from a lunatic asylum.

"We're geeks! Don't you see that?"

"Come on, Jack," Brady said. "I'll loan you my magic broadsword."

"I don't want a magic broadsword! I don't want extra hit points! I want a life! I want something real to happen to me!"

"Something drops on your head," said the Dungeon Master.

"You've been making so much noise that you didn't notice the giant spider slowly dropping toward you."

"Yeah, whatever."

"Before you can strike, it sinks its fangs into you." I heard dice rolling behind the screen. "Lose eighteen hit points."

"From one lousy spider bite?"

"It's a giant spider, Maximus," said Wolf Larson reasonably.

"I slice it in half with my sword," I said angrily. No way was I going to be eaten by a big bug on a Friday night.

"It's nimble," said the Dungeon Master. "It jumps higher along its thread, and then drops back down at you."

"I attack again!" I looked at the other players. "Aren't you guys gonna help me out here?"

"I'm in a pit," Van Doom said.

"You manage to chop off a couple of its legs," said the Dungeon Master, rolling, "but it strikes again. You lose another twelve hit points. . . ." More dice clattered against the tabletop. "And unfortunately its venom has entered your bloodstream. Roll a twenty-sided."

I rolled a two. All the other players were silent.

"You're dead," said the Dungeon Master.

"I can't be dead! I've got psionic powers and stuff."

"You never said you were using them."

"Well, obviously, I'd use them if I were fighting for my life."

The Dungeon Master just shrugged.

"Where's it say I'm dead?" I demanded. I stood up and came around the table to where the Dungeon Master sat.

"Nowhere," he said. "Anything can happen. That's what makes it so great."

Behind the screen were all his maps and notes—and his dice. I'd never seen so many dice before in my life. It was like a treasure trove. They were all different colors, translucent.

"So what happens now?" I asked.

"The game goes on."

"Without me."

"We might find a potion or a healer who can bring you back from the dead," Racknor said.

"Expensive," said Van Doom from his pit.

"Yeah, resurrection potions always are," said Racknor solemnly. "But stick around if you want. We might find something before long."

"No, I should get going."

Brady walked me to the door. "We play every Friday," he said.

"Yeah, maybe," I said. I doubted I'd be back, but on my way home, I kept thinking about the Dungeon Master's dice—how they'd glittered in the dim light like gemstones.

Biography:

Grew up: Port Alberni and Victoria on Vancouver Island, British Columbia, and Halifax, Nova Scotia, Canada

Now lives: Toronto, Canada

Random fact: Went through a video game addiction at fourteen but luckily got his first book out of it

Selected Bibliography:

Firewing

Sunwing

Airborn

DAVID SHANNON
No, David!

I made the original version of *No, David!* when I was about five years old. It was just drawings of me doing things I wasn't supposed to do, and the only words in the whole book were "no" and "David"—those were the only words I knew how to spell.

The drawing on the right is from the original version. It's a picture of me standing on a chair so I can snitch some cookie dough from the mixing bowl. I still think cookies taste better *before* they're baked!

My mom saved the book and showed it to me a few years ago. I thought it might make a good children's book, so I added a few more words and made some new drawings. At first I drew David with all my fancy high-falutin' professional art school training and he looked just like a real boy. But he wasn't nearly as funny as the original. So then I tried drawing him like I was still five years old, only better. I drew him standing on his chair again, and gave him scribbly eyes and pointy teeth and fingers, and I put lots of really breakable things on the shelves. And then David was a lot funnier. That's the picture on the left.

I sure am glad my mom saved that old book!

Biography:

Grew up: Spokane, Washington
Now lives: Los Angeles, California
Random fact: Likes to fish and play guitar, but not at the same time

Selected Bibliography:

No, David!
David Goes to School
David Gets in Trouble

The original No, David! *drafted by the artist at age five.*

JERRY PALLOTTA

Dead Body

When I was a young boy, our family spent every summer on Peggotty Beach in Scituate, Massachusetts. It was a great place to grow up. Our beach had everything—crabs, sharks, dolphins, seals, periwinkles, clams, mussels, starfish, limpets, chitons, mackerels, eels, and lobsters. There was even a day when a whale swam close to shore. My brothers, cousins, and I were never bored. Every day was an adventure!

I learned about fishing, harvesting seaweed, lobstering, clamming, surfing, and waterskiing. I also learned that in our New England ocean waters, there is not much that can hurt you. There are no deadly sea snakes or stonefish. Thank God there are no box jellies or electric eels, and no one in our sleepy ocean town has ever been bitten by a shark. At our beach, the only dangerous thing is the occasional piece of broken glass hidden under the sand.

But . . .

We do have ten-foot tides. A half mile to the south is the mouth of the North River. This area can be very dangerous. Very dangerous! You can see the fierce current between tides as the nun and can buoys almost get pulled underwater. It is especially treacherous when there is a combination of strong tidal current, big waves going in the opposite direction, and heavy crosswinds. Sometimes the water gets so foamy that if you fell in it, you wouldn't be able to float and you couldn't breathe, either. Every year someone drowns there. It is mostly inexperienced boaters, drunks, or know-it-all idiots who don't wear their life jackets.

One morning when I was ten years old, I was walking down the beach looking for a sea turtle. On the radio in between Beatles and Beach Boys songs, I had heard special reports that a leatherback turtle, the largest species of sea turtle, had been seen swimming nearby on Cape Cod.

I couldn't believe my luck. I saw something bobbing in the water close to shore. I looked and squinted through the sun reflections dancing on the surface of the water. I waded out knee-deep. I looked some more; I was convinced it was a sea turtle even though I had never seen one at our beach. As I got closer, now waist-deep, I couldn't believe what I saw. Suddenly, I had a sick taste in my mouth and almost threw up.

I ran home as fast as I could.

Mom! Mom! Dead body!

Mom! Mom! Dead body!

"Yeah right," said my mom as she was making coffee.

Mom! Mom! A dead body!

Mom, a real dead body!

"Yeah right," said my mom. My brothers and I were always goofing off. I guess she didn't believe me. She called our next-door neighbor, Mr. Romano, who was seventy-five years old.

"Go up the beach," she said. "Find out what this kid is up to."

Mr. Romano followed me up the beach. Then he frowned and his face turned spooky white. I was right; it was a dead body! Then it dawned on me; six weeks ago someone had drowned at the North River. Actually, two kids and a guy drowned. The Coast Guard found the two kids right away. Typical—no life jackets. How stupid! The guy was never found. Now here he was, almost right at my front door.

Mr. Romano walked back up the sand dunes to my house. "Mary, it is a dead body! Call the police!"

"Call the Coast Guard," I said.

The policemen and the Coast Guard guys arrived a few minutes later.

From the clothes, the dead body looked like a man, but it was floating facedown. The police asked us to row our dory close and push the dead body onto the beach. We were scared but we did it.

Once ashore, the police lifted the body, and the head fell off. Then I took a look at the hands. They were missing. Fish and crabs must have eaten them. All I saw were bones sticking out of his sleeves.

I had never seen a dead body before. No one in my family had ever died. No friends had ever died, either. I was not crying, but I knew something inside of me was different.

For the first time ever, I wondered what it would be like to be dead. Would it hurt? Would it be like sleeping?

The police told us that a human body sinks when it drowns, but six weeks later it floats. It floats because it starts to rot and decay and the decay turns our flesh into gas. I wondered what it would be like to rot and decay. Would I feel it?

I immediately thought of George O'Neil's smelly lobster bait that he left out one week. When I took the lid off the bait, I was almost knocked over by the disgusting smell. The rotten stinky bait was all flies and thousands—no, millions—of maggots. Maggots were everywhere. Is that what would happen to me if I didn't wear my life jacket? Would I drown, rot, and be reduced to maggots?

What a thought! That is what I was thinking as the police put the body in a body bag and hauled it away.

Biography:

Grew up: Medford and Scituate, Massachusetts

Now lives: In Red Sox Nation

Random fact: Has four brothers, two sisters, and seventy-two first cousins

Selected Bibliography:

The Victory Garden Vegetable Alphabet Book with Bob Thomson, illustrated by Edgar Stewart

The Icky Bug Alphabet Book illustrated by Ralph Masiella

The Bird Alphabet Book illustrated by Edgar Stewart

CHRISTOPHER PAOLINI
It All Began with Books

*It was also in her [Skadi's] terms of settlement that the Æsir were to do
something that she thought they would not be able to, that was to make
her laugh. Then Loki did as follows: he tied a cord round the beard of
a certain nanny-goat and the other end round his testicles, and they
drew each other back and forth and both squealed loudly. Then Loki
let himself drop into Skadi's lap, and she laughed.*

Can you guess where this piece comes from? The latest
gross-out comedy movie? Jim Carrey does fantasy? No? How
about this one:

*They moved down towards the frozen arch at great speed.
Skarphedin jumped up as soon as he tied his shoe and had his axe
raised. He ran to the river, but it was so deep that for a long stretch it
was unfordable. A broad slab of ice, smooth as glass, had formed on
the other side of the river, and Thrain and his men were standing in the
middle of it. Skarphedin took off into the air and leaped across the river
from one ice ledge to the other and made a steady landing and shot on
in a glide. The ice slab was very smooth, and Skarphedin went along
as fast as a bird in flight.*

*Thrain was about to put on his helmet, but Skarphedin came at
him first and swung his axe at him and hit him on his head and split it
down to the jaw, so that the molars fell out on the ice. This happened
in such rapid sequence that no one could land a blow on Skarphedin;
he went gliding away at a furious speed. Tjorvi threw a shield in his*

*way, but he hopped over it and kept his balance and glided to the end
of the ice slab. Then Kari and the others came up to him.*

"A manly attack, that!" said Kari.

Bad fantasy from someone who's read too much Conan the
Barbarian? The script to the next big action movie? A rip-off of
The Lord of the Rings?

Actually, none of those. The first excerpt is from Snorri
Sturluson's *Edda*, written in A.D. 1220, and the second from
Njal's Saga, written in A.D. 1280. As you can see, classical literature can be every bit as crude, bloody, exciting, and downright
entertaining as anything you'll find on TV or in the theater.

I grew up reading folklore, fairy tales, and other mythological
stories. The first fantasy book that I ever read was *The Ruby
Knight*, by David Eddings, the second book of his Elenium trilogy. *The Ruby Knight* had everything that a boy could want: sword-
fights, monsters, magic, true love, and terrible villains.

From that moment onward, I was hooked on fantasy. I
devoured the work of great authors, like Anne McCaffrey's
Dragonriders of Pern series, *Magician* by Raymond E. Feist, the
Earthsea trilogy by Ursula K. Le Guin, the Mossflower series by
Brian Jacques, *The Lord of the Rings* by J. R. R. Tolkien, the His
Dark Materials trilogy by Philip Pullman, and many, many more.

Eventually, I decided that I should try to expand my knowl-
edge and read some classic fantasy. Thus I quickly chewed
through—among others—the Gormenghast trilogy by Mervyn
Peake, *The Worm Ouroboros* by E. R. Eddison, and *The King of
Elfland's Daughter* by Lord Dunsany. Before I knew it, I had
worked my way back to ancient Nordic and Germanic epics,
where I made a shocking discovery: they're fun to read!

Yes, stuff written hundreds and even thousands of years ago is
fun! Read the Seamus Heaney translation of *Beowulf*. It has the
monster Grendel, a thrilling underwater fight, and an ancient
dragon. Tolkien loved *Beowulf* so much, he based parts of *The

Hobbit on it. In fact, Gandalf is named after a Norse dwarf. If you find *Beowulf* too hard, try *The 13th Warrior* by Michael Crichton, which retells the same story in a modern novel.

I loved the soaring adventure in those books, the way they could transport me into another world, where anything was possible. I dreamed about dropping out of school and grabbing a hatchet, a bow and arrow, and a backpack and just marching off into the mountains to find a quest of my own. I believed that life really was like a storybook and that when I grew up, I could do all the things I had read about.

And you know what? I was right.

Now that's not to say that I go around fighting monsters. However, I have had an incredible series of adventures because of what I read growing up. I taught myself to make knives and swords—I even built a forge for myself—I climbed local mountains, and, eventually, I wrote my own story, *Eragon*, which has taken me all around the world.

And it all began with books!

Sources: Sturluson, Snorri. *Edda.* Translated and edited by Anthony Faulkes. Everyman's Library, 1995. • *Njal's Saga.* Translated and edited by Robert Cook. Penguin Classics, 2002.

Biography:

Grew up: Paradise Valley, Montana
Now lives: Paradise Valley, Montana
Random fact: Hand-dug an eight-foot-deep hobbit hole in his backyard and topped it with an old satellite dish and dry grass

Selected Bibliography:

Eragon

GARY PAULSEN

from How Angel Peterson Got His Name

I had written a book about my life with my cousin Harris and talked about Harris peeing on an electric fence. The shock made him do a backflip and he swore he could see a rainbow in the pee. Many readers, especially women, were amazed that a boy would be insane enough to do this and didn't believe that it had happened. However, I did get many letters from men saying that either they or a brother or cousin or friend had tried the same stunt, with some exciting results. One man said it allowed him to see into the past.

I was sitting writing one day when my son, then thirteen, came into the house with a sheepish look on his deathly pale face. As he passed me, I couldn't help noticing that he was waddling.

"Are you all right?" I asked.

He nodded. "Sure. . . ."

"Why are you walking so funny?"

"Oh, no reason. I was doing something out by the goat barn and thought I'd try a little experiment. . . ."

"Pee on the electric fence?"

He studied me for a moment, then nodded. "How did you know?"

"It's apparently genetic," I said, turning back to work. "It's something some of us have to do. Like climbing Everest."

"Will I ever stop doing things like this?"

And I wanted to lie to him, tell him that as he grew older he would become wise and sensible, but then I thought of my own life: riding Harley motorcycles and crazy horses, running Iditarods, sailing single-handed on the Pacific.

I shook my head. "It's the way we are."

"Well," he sighed, tugging at his pants to ease the swelling, "at least I know what *that's* like and don't have to pee on any more fences."

And he waddled into his room.

Biography:

Grew up: Minneapolis, Minnesota

Now lives: In a house in New Mexico, and on a boat in the Pacific Ocean

Random fact: Ran away from home at age fourteen and traveled with a carnival

Selected Bibliography:

Hatchet

Harris and Me

How Angel Peterson Got His Name and Other Outrageous Tales about Extreme Sports

RICHARD PECK
The 1928 Packard

The other day I was making a speech somewhere about being a writer. Afterward, an old gent in a slouch hat came up. He'd brought his grandson, who he said was a faithful reader of my books.

"Do you have time for a story?" the grandfather asked. Of course I had time for a story. I'm a writer. His gaze grew filmy, and his grandson looked like he was about to hear a tale he'd heard before. "At around fourteen I was a handful," the old gent said. "So you know how busy I was around Halloween.

"My dad drove a 1942 Buick Eight."

I stirred. I too was from a world where a man was known by what he drove.

"At the other end of our street, a beat-up old 1928 Packard coupe was always parked at the curb, big as a Tiger tank."

He had my full attention now.

"I ought to have known better," he said, "but I dearly loved pinning horns." Pinning car horns was a sacred Halloween ritual. If you could get into a car, you jammed one end of a stick into the horn and wedged the other end against the back of the driver's seat. Then you ran like the devil, and the owner had to come out and unstick the horn before the battery ran down.

Horns went off all over town on Halloween, like car alarms do every night now.

"I skulked up the dark street," the old gent said, "and like a miracle the front window of the Packard was down. Why didn't this look too good to be true? I guess because I was fourteen."

I hung on his every word now, though his grandson's mind was wandering.

"I had me a stick just the right length. All I had to do was reach in the car window with it. I didn't even have to open the door. When I leaned inside with the stick, a hand shot up from the dark, and a fist the size of a ham grabbed my wrist. My heart stopped. I haven't been that scared since. The Packard's owner sat up in the seat and said, 'What can I do for you, son?'

"'You can turn me loose,' I said when I could breathe, and in three minutes I was back home in bed. I guess you know who the Packard belonged to."

I did. It was my dad's. Who else would own a twenty-year-old Hummer-esque Packard coupe for a fishing car? Who but my dad would lie all Halloween evening across the broken springs of its seat, waiting to catch a Halloweener just for the fun of it? And why couldn't the neighborhood kids remember that my dad looked forward to Halloween more than they did?

It was Skippy Oglesby my dad nabbed that particular Halloween night: Skippy Oglesby, the nearest thing our neighborhood had to a bully. And there he was again all these years and miles later, disguised by time as somebody's doting grandfather, to tell me another story about my dad.

And why not? My father was the perfect dad; he thought like a kid, but he was bigger than a bully. In fact, he was larger than life, older than the other dads but weirdly young, with a shoulder bunged up in World War I, and a Harley-Davidson he rode to work on mornings the Packard's engine wouldn't turn over. A big guy with a big grin and lures on his fishing hat.

Everything I write is an homage to him. Some of my stories are woven out of his memories. Some are memories of him. And some are things that didn't happen to him—to us—and I wish they had. But everything I write invites him back. Nobody a writer ever loved is dead.

Biography:
Grew up: Decatur, Illinois
Now lives: New York City
Random fact: Used to be a lecturer on cruise ships, and has been through the Panama Canal more times than he can count

Selected Bibliography:
A Long Way from Chicago
A Year Down Yonder
Past Perfect, Present Tense: New and Collected Stories

DANIEL PINKWATER
Lone ★ Ranger

Sometimes my mother would travel on business on behalf of my father. Usually she would go someplace and collect, or deliver, a thick envelope. Often I went with her. I think the idea was that a woman with a child would be less suspect—and she could carry out her errand while my father was in Chicago, being watched.

On one occasion—I was quite small—my mother and I took a train to some little Midwestern town. It was a dusty, wind-blown place . . . a single street, with a few buildings—a shabby hotel where we stayed, the grocer's, the cafe, the hardware store. I loved it! It was exactly like the Western towns in the movies!

And, to make it perfect, at one end of the main drag was a corral! It was a cattle pen, actually, I suppose—a vacant lot with a rough wooden fence around it—but it was cowboy enough for me. And it was being put to an unusual use that day. There was a banner strung above the lot. It read, MEET THE LONE ★ RANGER! TODAY ONLY AT 2:00 PM. There was some sort of rodeo in town, for the day, and he was the guest of honor.

Talk about a fortunate coincidence! The Lone Ranger was the greatest of all radio cowboys, and my personal hero. I was the Lone Ranger's biggest, most ardent, most crazed fan! I told my mother that she *had* to take me to see the Lone Ranger. It was too important for any discussion or argument. This was the astonishing, next-to-impossible chance of a lifetime. To see the Lone Ranger . . . in person . . . in some little burg in Indiana or Iowa . . . I didn't even know where we were. . . . It was too good, more than some mere coincidence. . . . Fate was at work here. And it was just across the street. She had to take me.

My mother was a woman of fashion and elegance. Her traveling ensemble—including tiny high heels, a mink jacket, a hat with a little veil, gloves—was not exactly suitable attire for attending a bucking horse contest. But she was going through with it. My intensity and earnestness had persuaded her that this was something she had to do as a mother.

So, under a threatening sky, at a little before two, we crossed the street, and my mother and I picked our way—she in her high-heeled shoes—through the feed lot, toward the small set of sparsely occupied bleachers and the fence against which a group of Western types lounged . . . including the Lone (Star) Ranger.

It seems that the five-pointed star painted on the banner between the words "Lone" and "Ranger" was not merely an element of decoration, but part of the name. It was not the Lone Ranger, as known and loved on radio, but some other ranger, Lone Star.

The Lone Star Ranger was small. His clothes were dirty. He had a two-day growth of beard. He had a mask, but it didn't fit well, and I could see that his eyes were quite red. He smelled of whiskey. And sweat. He didn't even have cowboy boots, but scuffed black oxfords. And instead of a pair of ivory-handled silver Colt peacemakers, he had an ordinary blue steel .38 like many of my father's friends.

Clearly, this wasn't the guy! I would have been sorely disappointed, but there wasn't time. Just as I was taking in the Lone Starness of this particular ranger, there was a stupendous cloudburst.

Instantly the surface of the lot turned from manure to liquid manure, the rain came down in drenching sheets, and my mother and I made for the hotel as best we could.

It was an awful experience, of course—but the Lone Star Ranger taught me a lesson, early in life, that many people never learn. It may not always be a good idea to meet your heroes close up and personal.

Biography:

Grew up: Memphis, Tennessee; Chicago, Illinois; and Los Angeles, California

Now lives: Dutchess County, New York

Random fact: While tending his organic garden, once came across an eggplant that bore a striking resemblance to Kurt Vonnegut

Selected Bibliography:

The Hoboken Chicken Emergency illustrated by Jill Pinkwater
Lizard Music
Blue Moose

DAVID SHELDON

I was nine years old when I drew "Batman Battles Superman." Even though Batman does not have superpowers, I thought he was obviously the big-time winner because of all the cool stuff he carried in his utility belt.

I wonder who would win the battle if Batman fought my newer illustration of the guy with the *big* hammer?

Selected Biography:

Grew up: Cincinnati, Ohio

Now lives: Kentucky

Random fact: Wanted to grow up to be a kangaroo because of the great pocket. Found out guy kangaroos don't have a pocket. Thought being a beaver might be cool. That didn't happen either.

Bibliography:

Pig Giggles and Rabbit Rhymes: A Book of Animal Riddles by Mike Downs

JACK PRELUTSKY
A Day at the Zoo

Okay . . . here's a true story from when I was about twelve or maybe fourteen years old. I never told it to my mother, because I'm sure she would have dropped dead on the spot. About a year later, I did tell my father, who rolled his eyes and thought it was sort of funny.

It all happened in the Bronx in the early 1950s. The Bronx is where I grew up and hung out with a guy named Bobby. We were great friends, because we had so much in common. Both of us could eat more of anything than anyone else we knew, and we were both experts at drinking milk and making it come out of our noses. We also got beat up by the same bigger kids.

The two of us also shared an interest in wild animals, and we were lucky to live just a couple of miles from the Bronx Zoo, one of the most famous zoos in the world. We went there often and always walked, not because we enjoyed walking all that much, but because we didn't have a whole lot of money. By saving on bus fare, we could afford to get a few hamburgers or hot dogs along the way. Then, while still digesting our food, we often worked on our belching technique.

Anyhow, it was the summer, and we were at the zoo. Both of us had cheap little cameras. I don't remember what Bobby's was, but mine was an old Kodak Brownie that my father had loaned me. It was a simple camera, good enough for taking close-ups of animals in cages, but practically useless for photographing anything at a distance.

We'd spent an hour or so snapping pictures of seals and leopards and keeping our distance from a certain famous monkey. The monkey was famous because he liked to throw his poop at people. His aim was pretty good . . . that's why we kept our distance. We decided to go over to an area called African Plains, a natural habitat ruled by lions, and without any ugly bars. A deep, very steep moat was the only barrier that kept the lions away from the folks visiting the zoo.

I took a few pictures of the lions, but felt frustrated because my little camera made the lions look like featureless clumps of tawny lint. I tried figuring out ways of getting closer . . . a lot closer. It occurred to me that if I went down into the moat, I'd get *really* close to the lions. There were numerous signs advising not to do this, but I paid them no attention. Bobby watched, with what I took to be admiration, as I climbed over the short fence, crossed a short level expanse, and slid down a practically vertical wall into the moat. As soon as I was at the bottom, I began snapping photos of the lions. *This was great!* They were so close now that I was getting some really good pictures, the best I'd ever taken. I was so involved with what I was doing that I failed to notice that several of the lions had taken an interest in me, and were casually inching toward the moat.

That's when a zookeeper, on the point of hysteria, suddenly appeared at the top of the wall. He screamed so loud that he startled me out of my photographic reverie. "What the hell are you doing down there? Are you crazy? Get back up here you idiot, and I mean *now!*"

I looked up at him, and replied innocently, "Why? The lions can't come down here. I'm safe. I'm OK."

The zookeeper screamed even louder. "No, you're not. They

can't climb up this side, but they can get down to where you are. . . . And they haven't been fed yet!"

A chill ran down my spine as I looked behind me and saw one of the lions leisurely sauntering down into the moat, heading in my direction. I wondered if he could smell the burgers on my breath. Suddenly, I was so scared that I began to belch uncontrollably. Still belching, I managed somehow to claw my way up the top of the wall in a fraction of the time it had taken me to get down. . . . I'd never moved so fast in my life. The zookeeper grabbed me by the collar and pulled me back over the fence.

He gave me a dirty look and said, "You've got to be the dumbest kid I've ever seen. Now get out of here. . . . I don't want to see you again." By way of an exclamation point, he added a not-so-little slap to the side of my head.

I took his advice without saying a word and left, noticing that Bobby couldn't stop laughing. On our way home I swore him to secrecy.

And that's just *one* story I never told my mother.

Biography:

Grew up: The Bronx, New York

Now lives: Washington State

Random fact: Has been a cab driver, furniture mover, and folk singer

Selected Bibliography:

The New Kid on the Block illustrated by James Stevenson

Ride a Purple Pelican illustrated by Garth Williams

It's Raining Pigs & Noodles illustrated by James Stevenson

JACK PRELUTSKY
Boys Are Big Experts

Boys are big experts
At looking for trouble,
They climb over fences,
They tunnel though rubble.
Boys take their time
When they're called to the table,
Boys have to eat
Like they live in a stable.

Boys love to throw things
And get into tussles,
Make nasty noises,
And show off their muscles,
Lots of stuff leading
To bruises and bleeding,
Why don't they stop for a while . . .
And start READING.

RICK REILLY

"Funny You Should Ask"
from The Life of Reilly

APRIL 12, 1999—So we were lying on our backs on the grass in the park next to our hamburger wrappers, my fourteen-year-old son and I, watching the clouds loiter overhead, when he asked me, "Dad, why are we here?"

And this is what I said.

"I've thought a lot about it, son, and I don't think it's all that complicated. I think maybe we're here just to teach a kid how to bunt, turn two, and eat sunflower seeds without using his hands.

"We're here to pound the steering wheel and scream as we listen to the game on the radio, twenty minutes after we pulled into the garage. We're here to look all over, give up, and then find the ball in the hole.

"We're here to watch, at least once, as the pocket collapses around John Elway, and it's fourth-and-never. Or as the count goes to three and one on Mark McGwire with bases loaded, and the pitcher begins wishing he'd gone on to med school. Or as a little hole you couldn't get a skateboard through suddenly opens in front of Jeff Gordon with a lap to go.

"We're here to wear our favorite sweat-soaked Boston Red Sox cap, torn Slippery Rock sweatshirt, and the Converses we lettered in, on a Saturday morning with nowhere we have to go and no one special we have to be.

"We're here to rake on a jack-high nothin' hand and have nobody know it but us. Or get in at least one really good brawl, get a nice shiner, and end up throwing an arm around the guy who gave it to us.

"We're here to shoot a six-point elk and finally get the f-stop right, or to tie the perfect fly, make the perfect cast, catch absolutely nothing, and still call it a perfect morning.

"We're here to nail a yield sign with an apple core from half a block away. We're here to make our dog bite on the same lame fake throw for the gazillionth time. We're here to win the stuffed bear or go broke trying.

"I don't think the meaning of life is gnashing our bicuspids over what comes after death, but tasting all the tiny moments that come before it. We're here to be the coach when Wendell, the one whose glasses always fog up, finally makes the only perfect backdoor pass all season. We're here to be there when our kid has three goals and an assist. And especially when he doesn't.

"We're here to see the Great One setting up behind the net, tying some poor goaltenders's neck into a Windsor knot. We're here to watch the Rocket peer in for the sign, two out, bases loaded, bottom of the career. We're here to witness Tiger's lining up the twenty-two-foot double breaker to win and not need his autograph afterward to prove it.

"We're here to be able to do a one-and-a-half for our grand-kids. Or to stand at the top of our favorite double-black on a double-blue morning and overhear those five wonderful words: 'Highway's closed. Too much snow.' We're here to get the Frisbee to do things that would have caused medieval clergymen to burn us at the stake.

"We're here to sprint the last hundred yards and soak our shirts and be so tired we have to sit down to pee.

"I don't think we're here to make *SportsCenter*. The really good stuff never does. Like leaving Wrigley at four fifteen on a perfect summer afternoon and walking straight into Murphy's with half of section 503. Or finding ourselves with a free afternoon, a little red 327 fuel-injected 1962 Corvette convertible, and an unopened map of Vermont's backroads.

"We're here to get the triple-Dagwood sandwich made, the perfectly frosted malted-beverage mug filled, and the football kicked off at the very second your sister begins tying up the phone until Tuesday.

"None of us are going to find ourselves on our deathbeds saying, 'Dang, I wish I'd spent more time on the Hibbings account.' We're going to say, 'That scar? I got that scar stealing a home run from Consolidated Plumbers!'

"See, grown-ups spend so much time doggedly slaving toward the better car, the perfect house, the big day that will finally make them happy when happy just walked by wearing a bicycle helmet two sizes too big for him. We're not here to find a way to heaven. The way is heaven. Does that answer your question, son?"

And he said, "Not really, Dad."

And I said, "No?"

And he said, "No, what I meant is, why are we here when Mom said to pick her up forty minutes ago?"

POSTSCRIPT: *Sometimes, you write a column and never hear another word about it—not from friends, not from strangers, not from anybody. But this one seems to have pierced a soft spot on people. To this day, I still get people telling me they faxed it to their kids, their parents, and their twenty best friends. People wrote their own columns about why we're here and sent them to me. I even turned it into a speech. If there's one column I'd like to be remembered, it's this one.*

Biography:

Grew up: Boulder, Colorado

Now lives: Denver, Colorado

Random fact: While coaching Little League, was upset about the lousy field the kids had to practice on. Built them a new field and called it Fishack Field. "Fishack"? An old slang word for sportswriter.

Selected Bibliography:

Missing Links

The Life of Reilly: The Best of Sports Illustrated's *Rick Reilly*

Who's Your Caddy?: Looping for the Great, Near Great, and Reprobates of Golf

PETER SÍS

Biography:

Grew up: Prague, Czech Republic

Now lives: Irvington, New York

Random fact: Used to be a dj in the Czech Republic and was the *first* dj in Poland

Selected Bibliography: *Trucks Trucks Trucks* • *Scranimals* by Jack Prelutsky • *The Tree of Life: Charles Darwin*

DAVID RICE
The Death of a Writer

In fourth grade our English teacher, Ms. Ayala, wanted us to write a short story. She said the best story would win a bag of pan dulce. When she said that, every kid in the class smiled with wide eyes. It had to be a story like Robinson Crusoe. We had to pretend we were shipwrecked on a deserted island, and then describe what we would do.

It was hard for us to imagine, because none of us had ever been on a ship and the only island we had been on was Padre Island. But Ms. Ayala said, "That's what imagination is for. You can write anything you want."

"Anything?" we asked.

"Yes, anything," she said with a warm, trusting smile.

I thought about it all morning and during lunch. In the playground, my friends and I were playing marbles, and all I could talk about was the story we had to write. Ramiro Ramos, who was burning ants with matches he snuck into school, looked up from his favorite hobby. "You heard her. She said we could write about anything we want. We can't get in trouble for writing what we want to write," he said as ants curled to the hot flame.

A few days later, our teacher started inviting students to read their stories out loud in front of the class. I can't remember any of them, not even my own, but I do remember Ramiro's.

When she called him, he got up and walked in front of the class and took out a folded sheet of paper from his back pocket. He unfolded it several times and cleared his throat. "This is my story," he said. "One day I was on a ship and it crashed on an island. There was this monster and it ate me. The End."

I started laughing because I thought it was the funniest story ever, but the other students looked confused. Ms. Ayala got mad and sent Ramiro to the principal's office, and he was paddled three times.

Biography:

Grew up: Edcouch, Texas
Now lives: Austin, Texas
Random fact: Drove a school bus for four years

Selected Bibliography:

Crazy Loco
Give the Pig a Chance & Other Stories

STEVE RUSHIN
Sweet Dreams

In high school I sat in the basement and watched Minnesota Twins games on TV and wrote earnest stories about them on my mom's Royal typewriter. You had to strike the keys violently—as if trying, on a carnival midway, to ring a bell with a sledgehammer. The keys went *bang!* and the carriage-return bell went *ping!* and I dreamed, absurdly, of writing for *Sports Illustrated*.

This dream may not sound like much to you, and I sometimes feel like Lily Tomlin, who said, "I always wanted to be somebody, but I should have been more specific." More often, though, I recognize that herein lies the central beauty of sports: lifelong dreams are fulfilled every day. Few fantasize about careers in waste management or systems analysis or double-entry book-keeping, fulfilling as those jobs may turn out to be.

But in sports, every day, someone realizes his once-ridiculous ambition of getting green-blazered at Augusta or fulfills his absurd childhood fantasy by stepping to the plate in a major league baseball game. We spend so much time cautioning kids not to dream of playing big league ball—"There are only seven hundred jobs"—that we often forget a salient point: there are seven hundred jobs, and they have to be filled by real people, most of whom are thankful that nobody crushed out their dreams like a spent Camel. Hope, a philosopher said, is the dream of the waking.

"Try some more," said another great thinker, Willie Wonka, while urging the brats who toured his chocolate factory to sample the lickable wallpaper. "The strawberries taste like strawberries! The snozzberries taste like snozzberries!"

"Snozzberries?!" replied Veruca Salt. "Whoever heard of a snozzberry?"

To which Wonka said only, "We are the music-makers. And we are the dreamers of dreams."

He was alluding to a nineteenth-century poet named Arthur O'Shaughnessy, who wrote:

We are the music-makers,
And we are the dreamers of dreams,
Wandering by lone sea-breakers,
And sitting by desolate streams;
World-losers and world-forsakers,
On whom the pale moon gleams:
Yet we are the movers and shakers
Of the world forever, it seems.

The world belongs to those who see its possibilities. Dreaming is like believing in God or enrolling in the United frequent-flier program: it costs nothing, yet has potentially transcendent rewards. Why not dream? Yours can be audaciously gigantic: a teenage Ted Williams, after all, dreamed of people seeing him and saying, "There goes Ted Williams, the greatest hitter who ever lived." (Now, remarkably, they do just that.)

Or your dream can be laughably humble. Seven years after I graduated from high school, the Twins won Game 7 of the World Series at the Metrodome, and I drove a rental car through downtown Minneapolis to my childhood home in the suburbs, where I wrote, in the basement, the story for *Sports Illustrated*.

The dream fulfilled is every bit as fantastic as I once imagined it to be. The strawberries really do taste like strawberries. And the snozzberries taste like snozzberries.

Biography:

Grew up: Born in Chicago, grew up in Bloomington, Minnesota

Now lives: New York City

Random fact: Used to sell hot dogs at the stadium during Twins and Viking games

Selected Bibliography:

Road Swing: One Fan's Journey into the Soul of America's Sports
The Caddie Was a Reindeer and Other Tales of Extreme Recreation

RENÉ SALDAÑA, JR.

Maybe Yeah, Maybe Nah

"So, you gonna call the cops on me, or what?" asked Miguel, his oversized, shiny Dallas Cowboys jacket bulging in places.

The old man, the Don Fonti of the sign on the store window, stood behind the counter, his forehead wrinkled—thinking real hard. He even sighed, then said, "Maybe."

The boy shook his head slightly, wondered if he should make a run for it. The geezer would have to come out from behind the counter, then run, and he was older than spit, so Miguel could make it out the door easy, then down the street, then stop somewhere—at the park, or in some alley—and there he'd pull out the soda pop that was making his armpit freeze and get out all the other stuff to eat. "What d'yuh mean 'maybe'?" he said, and looked Don Fonti straight on.

"Maybe you've learned your lesson today?—then I won't. Maybe you haven't?—I will. It's all on you, little man."

The boy thought some more, didn't like being called "little man," thought the old man would probably die of a heart attack or fall and break a hip if he even dared give chase. Worse came to worst and the geezer came close to catching up, he'd dump the stuff in some alley.

The old man kept looking at the boy, smack in the eyes, not turning away, but staring him down, like, *So what's it gonna be, son?*

The old man's arms dangled at his sides; not a care in the world, it seemed to Miguel.

"I'll tell you what too, son, just to complicate matters for you: I ain't running after you. I'm too old, and what you're taking's no skin off my nose."

Miguel looked over at the door, the little bell over it still, tied to a hook screwed over the threshold, considered running, but instead pulled the can of soda from inside the jacket, a bag of chips and some candy bars from the jacket pockets, and put them on the counter in front of the old man, though not letting go of the can just yet, still doing some hard thinking.

They were staring at each other again, then Miguel pushed the soda, candy, and chips at the old man, pushed hard, then said, "Maybe I have learned something, maybe I haven't. For me to know, you to find out. I know this much, though—you can stuff all that," he said, pointing at the goods. "Stuff all that up your big, hairy nose, geezer," and Miguel ran out of the store quick, shot out of there, not once looking back, not even one time. Just kept running until he was out of breath and far away from the store.

Finally he stopped—turned to see. But neither the old man nor anyone else had come after him. Only thing, out of breath like he was, his brain pounding at the temples, he could swear he still heard the bell dingling from down the street.

Biography:

Grew up: Peñitas, Texas

Now lives: Edinburg, Texas

Random fact: Now that he has a son, Lukas, he has a good excuse to be out in the open about collecting and playing with Hot Wheels cars

Selected Bibliography:

The Jumping Tree: A Novel
Finding Our Way

GRAHAM SALISBURY
Bufos

One sunny Kailua morning, my mom's boyfriend Ledward drove up in his beat-up truck. I was fishing for aholehole in the swampy canal that ran by our yard, using raw bacon for bait. It was peaceful, just me and my bamboo pole. I liked being alone.

But lately, my mom had been having secret talks with Ledward about me. One time I overheard her say, "He needs a man around the house," and, "Honestly, I just don't know what to do with him."

Ledward said, "Huh."

We did have this girl living with us—Stella, a high school junior from Texas. She said to me, "Your mom wants me to watch you, but you don't *even* know how hard that is, because you're a joke and you make me sick, you know?"

She was the joke. Where Mom found her, I didn't know. Under a rock, prob'ly.

Ledward, six-four in his bare feet, thumped the truck door shut and headed my way in his shorts and T-shirt.

Great, I thought. *Why don't you just go in and see Mom and leave me alone?*

"Fishing good?" he said, walking up, standing behind me.

"It's okay," I said, without turning around.

"You caught anyt'ing yet?"

"Nope."

"*Humph.*"

The swamp that day smelled like sulfur and rotting mud. I was thinking about going over to Willy's, maybe go to the beach, get away before my mom tried to make me do some work around the house.

A fat toad croaked in the deep lawn, then leaped out and headed toward the water. We called them bufos, short for bull-frog. They were everywhere in our yard.

Ledward said, "You know why you got bufos in da grass, boy?"

"No."

"You no cut da grass, hass why. You let um grow too long, ah? Bufos come inside, dig down. Dey like dat."

"I cut it."

"Yeah, but if you cut um more often dey no come, ah?"

"So?"

"Look bad, too, you no cut um. Make dis place look like a junkyard."

"So?"

"So go get da lawn mowah—go, I wait."

I looked back over my shoulder and squinted up at him. "Wait all day. You're not my boss."

"You t'ink?"

"Yeah."

I turned toward the canal. *Go away*, I thought. I should say that.

"Who going cut um, den? Your mama? Da girl?"

"Who cares who? All I know is you're not my boss."

"You like if I do it for you?"

"Do what you want."

"Hokay, no problem. . . . But boy . . ."

"What?"

"Afta I cut um dis one time you going do um ev'ry Sataday now on, ah? Keep um short so no bufos come inside. Make the yard look nice. One less problem for your mama."

"I said, you ain't my boss."

"No?"

"No."

"Huh. I guess nex' Sataday we going fine out, ah?"

I turned again to squint at him, the sun blazing over his shoulder. "What do you mean?"

"Sataday come, you no cut um, you going fine out."

"I'm telling Mom you threatened me."

"You call that one t'ret?"

"Yeah I call that a threat."

Ledward nodded. "Huh . . . but guess what."

"What."

"You ain't seen not'ing yet."

Biography:

Grew up: The Hawaiian Islands, his family having been there since 1820

Now lives: Portland, Oregon, a place so pure and clean it squeaks

Random fact: Flunked out of college, wrote and played music for five years, was motivated to go back to college, then graduated with honors

Selected Bibliography:

Shark Bait
Island Boyz
Lord of the Deep

LANE SMITH

"When I was a kid I always liked outer space stuff. Still do. . . ."

```
      Behind a rock was a giant dragonfly.  It almost
    stung Mr. Space, but he gave him a trick of his own.
    He shot him.
```

```
      Soon the only thing you could hear was,
    10--9--8--7--6--5--4--3--2--1--0--BLAST-OFF!
      Now he was in space.
```

Biography:

Grew up: Born in Tulsa, Oklahoma. Grew up in Corona, California.

Now lives: Connecticut

Random fact: Doesn't like coconut

Selected Bibliography:

The Happy Hocky Family!
The Happy Hocky Family Moves to the Country!
Pinocchio the Boy (or Incognito in Collodi)

JON SCIESZKA

Brothers

I grew up with five brothers. No sisters. I'm the second oldest of the Scieszka brothers—Jim, Jon, Tom, Gregg, Brian, Jeff. There were so many of us that even my dad had trouble remembering our names. He would call to one of us, "Jim . . . erhh, Tom . . . erhh, Jon . . . I mean . . . hey you."

Growing up, we brothers did a lot of "guy" things together. Without knowing anything different, we just figured everyone wrestled in their living room, played Cowboys and Indians with their babysitter (and maybe left her tied up in the closet just a little too long), fought dirt-clod wars in empty lots, built model airplanes (then lit them on fire and blew them up for more realistic crashes), collected every Hardy Boys book, read every Sgt. Rock comic, and watched every TV cartoon possible.

We also built forts, explored sewers, tracked rabbits in the snow, accidentally lit that dead tree in the park on fire, and shot a lot of things we probably shouldn't have shot with our BB guns. I learned to cook by cooking like my mom—in massive amounts. A pot of oatmeal still doesn't look quite right to me unless it's industrial size. And I still have a hard time roasting just one chicken. It looks so lonely.

We tied Tom into bed when we were babysitting. We broke

Gregg's collarbone at least three times playing football. We laughed at baby Brian playing in the toilet. We encouraged baby Jeff to eat plant dirt and cigarette butts for the entertainment of our friends. Well, didn't everyone do that with their brothers?

Brothers are a bit of a puzzle. They are the guys you would put in a headlock and try to ram through the bathroom door. But they are the same guys you wouldn't let anyone touch in a schoolyard recess rumble. Brothers are the guys you would tease without mercy. But they are also the same guys you wouldn't let anyone else in school bad-mouth.

Brothers are the guys you stick with and stick up for.

The Scieszka brothers are scattered all over the country now, but we still get together once a year to play a family golf tournament. We named it after our dad, Lou, and his favorite car—his old Cadillac Coupe de Ville. It is the Coupe de Lou Classic. We all grew up playing golf, because Dad Lou, an elementary school principal, taught Junior Golf and gave us lessons during summers off. And I'm sure my brothers would want me to point out the amazing fact that I am the winner of both the very first Coupe de Lou 1983 and the latest Coupe de Lou 2004.

But of all the Scieszka brother memories, I believe it was a family car trip that gave us our finest moment of brotherhood. We were driving cross-country from Michigan to Florida, all of us, including the family cat (a guy cat, naturally), in the family station wagon. Somewhere mid-trip we stopped at one of those Stuckey's rest-stop restaurants to eat and load up on Stuckey's candy.

We ate lunch, ran around like maniacs in the warm sun, then packed back into the station wagon—Mom and Dad up front, Jim, Jon, Tom, Gregg, Brian, Jeff, and the cat in back. Somebody dropped his Stuckey's Pecan Log Roll® on the floor. The cat found it and must have scarfed every bit of it, because two minutes later we heard that awful *ack ack ack* sound of a cat getting ready to barf.

The cat puked up the pecan nut log. Jeff, the youngest and smallest (and closest to the floor) was the first to go. He got one look and whiff of the pecan nut cat yack and blew his own sticky lunch all over the cat. The puke-covered cat jumped on Brian. Brian barfed on Gregg. Gregg upchucked on Tom. Tom burped a bit of Stuckey lunch back on Gregg. Jim and I rolled down the windows and hung out as far as we could, yelling in group puke horror.

Dad Lou didn't know what had hit the back of the car. No time to ask questions. He just pulled off to the side of the road. All of the brothers—Jim, Jon, Tom, Gregg, Brian, and Jeff—spilled out of the puke wagon and fell in the grass, gagging and yelling and laughing until we couldn't laugh anymore.

What does it all mean? What essential guy wisdom did I learn from this?

Stick with your brothers. Stick up for your brothers. And if you ever drop a pecan nut log in a car with your five brothers and your cat . . . you will probably stick to your brothers.

Biography:

Grew up: Michigan

Now lives: Brooklyn, New York

Random fact: Has been wondering, ever since kindergarten song time, if the hokey pokey really is what it's all about

Selected Bibliography:

The Stinky Cheese Man and Other Fairly Stupid Tales illustrated by Lane Smith

The Time Warp Trio series illustrated by Lane Smith (books 1–8), illustrated by Adam McCauley (books 9–14)

Science Verse illustrated by Lane Smith

DARREN SHAN

GUY
~~Manifesto~~—*Who We Are!*

Guys BURP! Burping is our way of communicating with each other. We can say just about anything we want with a good burp. Girls gossip—guys burp. If a girl complains about you burping, you should tell her, "I'll stop burping when you stop gossiping!"

Guys SCRATCH! Guys scratch themselves all over. It's how we check ourselves for wounds, insects, and all manner of other stuff. It goes back to when we were cavemen and didn't have any medicines. It's a natural defense and should be encouraged, not criticized.

Guys SNIFF! Often right after they SCRATCH. It keeps our nostrils in shape. This was very important in olden times, when a good set of nostrils was the best way of telling if there were any dangerous animals about.

Guys WRESTLE! It's a noble, ancient art. In Greek and Roman times, wrestlers were treated like heroes. Watching two grown men in tights throwing each other around a canvas ring is not silly or childish—it's our way of keeping alive glorious cultures and traditions.

Guys ARE HAIRY! Girls make us shave, but beards and mustaches are great—they give us a fierce yet dignified look. Abe Lincoln had a beard! So did most of the other great guys of history. Every guy has an obligation to grow a beard or mustache at least once in his life.

Guys LIKE SPORTS! Real guys know that jobs, wives, money, family, and all the rest are only background details. Sports are what we were born for, either as competitors or spectators. It doesn't matter whether it's football, basketball, baseball, or Ludo—all guys love some sort of a sport, more than they can ever love anything else (except perhaps their car or dog).

Guys BITE THEIR TOENAILS! This is an art form, not a disgusting habit! If Olympic gymnasts could bend down far enough to bite their toenails, they'd win gold medals every time! We defy the physical laws when we chew our toenails. Not only should we not stop doing it—we should do it more often, and in public!

After guys BITE THEIR TOENAILS THEY CHEW THE NAILS UP INTO LITTLE PIECES AND SWALLOW THEM! Not an art form, really, but crunchy—yum!

After guys BITE THEIR TOENAILS AND CHEW THEM UP AND SWALLOW THEM THEY FIND A GIRL AND KISS HER! Heh-heh-heh-heh-heh!

Guys DON'T COOK! Guys never cook, or do the washing-up, or even set foot in a kitchen unless it's to eat food that has already been prepared. Unless they're a famous chef. Then it's OK. Otherwise it's a major no-no! (Making popcorn doesn't count as cooking, and it's OK to BBQ, too. Anything else—nuh-uh!)

Making up a bed? Tidying a bedroom? **PUH-LEASE!**

Guys ALWAYS EAT WITH THEIR MOUTHS OPEN! It makes the food taste better, and when little bits fall out and get stuck in your sweater or T-shirt, you can spend many happy hours picking them out and finishing them off. Even yummier than toenails!

Guys DON'T WEAR SUITS! No where, no why, no how! Any guy who wears a suit is a slave to the man and no longer worthy of the honorable title of GUY! If you see a guy wearing a suit, you should report it at once to the F.G.I. (Federal Guy Investigators).

Guys NEVER KISS GIRLS! Unless they've bitten their toenails off (see above) or have just eaten a load of garlic, and want to make the girl suffer.

Guys DON'T DO PINK! It's not our color. Fact!

Guys DON'T GET UP EARLY! Unless it's for sports. And even then, we do so reluctantly, with much moaning and groaning.

Guys DON'T CARE ABOUT SCHOOLWORK! We do it to shut our parents up, sure, but we know it doesn't really matter, since we're all going to be rich, famous sports stars when we grow up.

And, finally, most important of all, guys FART! And real guys always call it FARTING! We don't "toot" or "break wind" or "have a little whistle." We f-a-r-t-FART! And we're proud of our farts! We are the master farters of the universe—louder, longer, and smellier than any other creature in the world! Girls envy us our flatulent abilities—that's why they constantly moan about them, to try to drag us down to their own mediocre level. You should never apologize for farting, or try to keep a fart bottled in. True guys fart anytime, anywhere, devil be damned! Yes, it's especially nice when we let off a loud, foul, juicy one underneath the covers late at night, then dip our heads beneath the sheets for a good, long SNIFF—but don't keep all those decadent smells for yourselves, guys! Because above all else, guys love to share, and farts are made to be shared with the world—especially girls!

N.B. This list is not exclusive—every guy should feel free to add to it, to expand and explore the boundaries of guydom. Then show it to your parents and teachers, to explain who you are and what you're made of. And if you fart on the paper just before handing it in, you might just get an extra couple of points—but only if your teacher is a GUY!

Biography:
Grew up: London, England, then Limerick, Ireland
Now lives: Limerick, Ireland
Random fact: Although he writes a lot about vampires, he unfortunately cannot help you turn into one

Selected Bibliography:
A Living Nightmare (Cirque Du Freak #1)
The Vampire's Assistant (Cirque Du Freak #2)
Tunnels of Blood (Cirque Du Freak #3)

ROBERT SIEGEL
The Day I Threw the Trivia Bowl

I have a confession to make: I threw the Trivia Bowl.

The year was 1988. The place, eleventh grade.

In 1988, as an academically advanced (read: geeky) sixteen-year-old, my primary objective in life was the maintenance of my low profile among classmates. I did not want to stick out in any way, especially for anything that had even the faintest whiff of dorkery.

Problem was, I happened to be the captain of a formidable four-man Trivia Bowl team that was to represent the school at the countywide Trivia Bowl competition. For a boy prone to nightmares of academic achievement–related mockery, this was not good.

The night before the Trivia Bowl, I was freaking. I imagined that if we won, they would proudly announce it over the intercom to the entire school during homeroom. This is what they did whenever someone did something notable. I imagined all the kids pointing and laughing at the trivia dork. This prospect terrified me beyond words.

And yet, another part of me desperately wanted to win the Trivia Bowl. I loved trivia and, even more, I loved winning at stuff. It was a terrible dilemma.

The day of the competition comes. We burst out of the gate strongly. What is the capital of Nepal? Kathmandu. What is the largest animal that has ever lived? The blue whale. By the end of the first round, we were in second place and, thanks to a furious late run, had momentum squarely on our side. I was excited, but all the while in the back of my mind, I was imagining that dreaded homeroom announcement.

Things go even better (or worse) in Round Two. We take the lead. As the competition heads toward the finish, it becomes clear that it's a two-team race. Us versus our hated rivals from Massapequa. We go back and forth, trading blows like Foreman and Ali.

It all comes down to one question. If we get it right, we win; if we miss, they have the chance to answer for the win.

"Who shot Robert F. Kennedy?"

Uh-oh. I know it.

No one else on my team knows. They all look at me expectantly. I am well-known amongst them as the assassination expert. They assume I will blurt out the answer, which, of course, is Sirhan B. Sirhan. I hem and haw. *What's going on?* they are clearly wondering. *Rob doesn't know?* After what seems like an eternity, I give my answer:

"Jack Ruby?"

"I'm sorry, that's not correct."

Massapequa pounces and gets it right. My teammates and I watch as they hold aloft the 1988 Trivia Bowl trophy in sweet victory.

The whole ride home, I wrestled with my decision to blow the Trivia Bowl. I felt terrible about what I did, but at least I would avoid homeroom humiliation. Right?

Wrong. The next morning in homeroom:

"Congratulations to eleventh-graders Robert Siegel, Mark

Roth, Adam Frankel, and Dan Eckert for their valiant effort yesterday in the countywide Trivia Bowl competition, in which they placed second."

Not only was I a dork, I was a losing dork.

The moral of the story is, if you're ever in a Trivia Bowl, don't throw it. Either way, they're gonna announce it in homeroom, so you might as well win.

Biography:

Grew up: Merrick, New York (Long Island)
Now lives: Manhattan
Random fact: Has never burped
Occupation: Former Editor in Chief of *The Onion*

Selected Bibliography:

Our Dumb Century: "The Onion" Presents 100 Years of Headlines from American's Finest News Source with The Onion, Inc.

Dispatches from the Tenth Circle: The Best of "The Onion" with The Onion, Inc.

"The Onion" Ad Nauseam news archives with The Onion, Inc.

RICK SPEARS

Bringing Up 'Saur Subjects

What is it with dinosaurs? Why are they so fascinating, especially to children? It was once said that kids are infected with a virus that makes them crazy for dinosaurs. Some of us, thankfully, never developed immunity to this dino-virus. If ever a cure is found, I don't want to know about it!

My earliest recollection concerning dinosaurs is a cool book my parents gave me all about prehistoric life. (Almost forty years later, I still have it.) I have been drawing dinosaurs as far back as I can remember. My parents tell me I went through a submarine phase for a bit, but promptly came back around to the ancient reptiles. This picture of a T. rex and a triceratops squaring off is typical of my nine-year-old abilities.

The animals' coloration (and the jagged teeth on the triceratops) probably came from the remote-controlled dinosaurs my younger brother and I received from Santa: a green T. rex and a brown triceratops. I am sure the river of lava I have shown them fighting next to was inspired by a dinosaur display I saw at Disneyland. No animals, prehistoric or modern, are going to hang around an erupting volcano, but it sure makes for an exciting composition!

As I grew up, other subjects moved to the forefront of my

Rick Spears, age nine

consciousness, namely girls and Star Wars (but not necessarily in that order). Dinosaurs, however, managed to still lurk around, as if waiting for their day. That day came in 1986 when, while working in an art studio just after college, I was given the task of drawing dinosaurs for an ad campaign.

I thought I was familiar enough with the subject, but I did some research anyway and was stunned by how much I didn't know! So I bought up every book I could find and fell in love with dinosaurs all over again. That project inspired me to start making 3-D models of dinosaurs. Some people that saw the models would ask me to build them some dinos, too.

So little by little, I got out of the ad business and into the museum business, and eventually turned my hobby of drawing and making models of dinosaurs into my career. All because of a book from my mom and dad, and an incurable case of dinosaur fever!

Biography:

Grew up: Born in California, but grew up in Georgia

Now lives: Georgia

Random fact: The largest model I have built (so far) was a life-size Tyrannosaurus rex (32 feet long) for a children's mall. Unfortunately the mall closed down, and the owners cut the dino's head off and threw away the body!

Selected Bibliography:

Dinosaur Mummies: Beyond Bare-Bones Fossils
by Kelly Milner Halls

SEYMOUR SIMON
Roy G. Biv

Roy G. Biv. Ever hear of him? He was a character in a story that I read many years ago when I was growing up in New York City. The story was in one of the SF pulp magazines published at that time: *Astounding Stories, Amazing Stories, Startling Stories, Thrilling Wonder Stories.* There may have been a fifth magazine, too, but I forgot its name.

When I was in first or second grade and just beginning to read on my own, my older cousin gave me a pile of old SF pulp magazines. He told me that "SF" was the abbreviation for "science fiction" and that pulp was the name of the rough cheap paper on which they were printed. It didn't make any difference to me that the paper was cheap; I loved reading the stories in those magazines.

The SF stories in those pulps were mostly about space travel (that was *way* before spaceships were sent to the moon and the planets). The stories also featured smart heroes who confronted and usually conquered dangerous BEMs. BEMs? Bug-eyed monsters, of course.

The action in the stories often took place on Mars, or on other planets in the solar system, or on planets circling stars far, far, away on the other side of the galaxy. Sometimes the action took place on Earth and sometimes even in a city named New

York. But it wasn't the New York City I knew. It was a New York in the distant future. A city that had private cars zooming around in the air, anti-gravity machines that allowed people to float around in space, and robots that did any chores that needed to be done. It was, in a word, *neat-o*.

I was mostly interested in the stories I was reading, but I picked up all kinds of other things along the way. I knew the names of all the planets and their moons. (Well, not *all* their moons, because a lot more moons have been discovered since then.) I knew the names of lots of stars, the difference between a galaxy and a star cluster, and why a laser gun needed to be recharged from time to time.

I don't remember most of the names of characters in the stories I used to read in those days. But I still remember Roy G. Biv. In the story, Roy was an alien who had come to this planet on a beam of light. And he had to choose a name for himself. I'll always remember the name he chose. Because *Roy G. Biv* is made from the first letters of the spectrum of colors that make up visible light: red, orange, yellow, green, blue, indigo, and violet. Roy G. Biv. See? Now you will remember his name and the colors of the spectrum as well. It's just astounding, amazing, and startling what a guy can pick up by reading.

Biography:
Grew up: New York City
Now lives: New York State
Random fact: Has written over two hundred books

Selected Bibliography:
Volcanoes
Sharks
Snakes

ARTHUR SLADE

The Hammer and the Bullet

It's fun having a big brother, right? I mean, yeah, they hold you down, spit on either side of your head, then threaten to drop a gob on your face, but that's all part of being a big brother. They also teach you things. My older brother, David, taught me all the different parts of a car engine. (I've since forgotten them, but at one point I did know.) He also taught me how to snare a gopher with bale twine. (I grew up on a ranch with five hundred cows and about five thousand gophers.) But there's one thing he showed me that I'll never forget.

One day David came into my room holding a tin pan. I was about ten or so, reading my *Spider-Man* comics and practicing my quick-witted Spider-Man quips. David strode up to me and said, "Watch this!" He set the pan on my bed and pulled a .22 shell out of his pocket and bit down on the head of the bullet. Any second I expected the bullet to go *bang!* and his head to disappear. Or at least his teeth. He kept working at it. Wow! He was eating a bullet. A second later he twisted the bullet head out of the shell and spat it into the pan. He then poured the gunpowder out of the shell into the tin, making a line. He produced a match, lit it, and my eyes widened as I watched a flame rush from one side of the tin to the other.

"That was the coolest thing I've ever seen!" I said, in awe. He really was an amazing big brother.

The next day, I decided to do the same thing. So I took a .22 bullet to my dad's shop and closed the door. I bit down on the bullet and tried to twist it out of the shell, but all I did was get sore teeth. My brother must have jaws of steel. The bullet did have imprints of my teeth, though. So next I put the .22 in the vice grip and tried to twist the top off with a pair of pliers. Most of the bullet came away, but half of it was left in the shell, so I couldn't get to the gunpowder. All I needed was a hole to pour the gunpowder out of. So, without thinking about the consequences, I grabbed a hammer and a nail and began to lightly tap the nail into the bullet. Nothing happened, but I did make a dent. So I leaned a little closer and hammered a bit harder. Nothing. At this point I became very stubborn. It occurred to me that I had to hit the nail even harder. So I swung and connected perfectly with the nail.

Bang!

The .22 shell exploded, what remained of the bullet shot into the air, narrowly missing my nose. It smacked a hole in the rafters. I dropped the hammer and held my hand, counting the fingers. One. Two. Three. Whew! There were four. And a thumb. Three fingers were bleeding where the metal of the exploded shell had torn into them. They were blackened by the gunpowder, too. I wrapped them up in a rag and put the hammer away. The nail was long gone. The bullet hole in the ceiling wasn't noticeable unless you looked directly at it. I threw the twisted remains of the shell away and proceeded home. I got three Band-Aids, covered my fingers, and held them out of sight for the next couple of days. I never did tell my parents. Nor did I ever figure out how my brother bit the head off a bullet. All I know is I won't try anything like it again.

Biography:

Grew up: Cypress Hills, Saskatchewan, Canada

Now lives: Saskatoon, Saskatchewan, Canada

Random fact: In all his time riding horses at the ranch where he grew up, he never wore a cowboy hat

Selected Bibliography:

Dust
Tribes

WILLIAM SLEATOR
The Masque of the Red Death

When I was a kid, some of the other guys made fun of me at school. They said I threw a ball like a girl. I was always the last one picked for teams. I was so used to it that it didn't bother me. I was always way out in left field or right field or whichever field it is that balls hardly ever go to, and I lived in fear that a ball would come my way and I'd have to try to catch the thing and it would hit me on the head or I'd drop it. PE was the worst thing about school.

But I loved playing the piano. I started lessons at eight and really took to it. By the time I was in sixth grade I was playing real music—Bach and Mozart. My father played the violin, and he and I really liked playing sonatas together. Our family always had a big Christmas Eve party and everybody would lean over around the grand piano and sing while I played carols.

I liked to make up music, too. One of my first pieces was called "Guillotines in the Springtime." Another one was called "A BM in the Snow." (If you don't know what "BM" means, ask around.) I studied the cello, too, and played in the school orchestra, and in eleventh grade I wrote a piece for the whole orchestra that we performed at an assembly. Some of the guys who made fun of me stood up and applauded at the end, and later I overheard one of them say, "You gotta respect somebody who can write music like that." They all thought I was a genius after that. I did nothing to correct this impression.

Senior year I was friends with some girls who were in modern dance, and we decided to put on a ballet that I would compose the music for. The modern dance teacher liked the idea. I picked a story by Edgar Allen Poe, "The Masque of the Red Death." The story is about a country where a terrible plague is going on, called the Red Death. Actually, it was sort of like the Ebola virus: when you died, blood gushed out of your pores, especially your face.

The prince wanted to avoid getting sick, so he invited his rich friends who were still healthy to stay in his most remote palace, and locked all the doors and sealed the gates shut so nobody with the disease could get in.

This palace had a peculiar suite of seven rooms. Each room was painted a particular color, and everything in the room was the same color, including the lighting. There was a blue room, a purple room, and so on. At the end was the black room, draped in black velvet, which had a huge ebony clock that struck the hours in a particularly gloomy way. In only this room was the lighting a different color from the walls: blood red.

The prince had a masked ball in this suite. Everyone wore bizarre costumes and masks, and danced. But every time the clock struck the hour, the music stopped and the people stopped dancing. When the clock struck midnight, a new figure appeared, a person in a costume that looked like somebody who had died of the Red Death, in a corpselike mask with blood coming from the pores. The prince was furious—the whole reason they were here was to avoid the Red Death—and chased the figure, who went into the black room. The prince lifted his knife to stab it, and there was nothing under the costume. Blood gushed from the prince's face, and he fell over dead from the disease. And then all the partygoers died of the Red Death.

Of course I loved this story—it was so inspiring! For the ballet, we simplified it and made only three rooms. It started normal and got weirder. The blue room was a waltz, the purple room was a tango, and the black room was spooky and dissonant. The sets were also very eerie. We really wanted to scare the audience. It took a lot of work and rehearsal to put it all together.

Unfortunately, my eccentric great-aunt Ronnie was sitting in the front row at the one performance. She was a scientist who had been a flapper in the 1920s and chain smoked well into her nineties. During the performance, when she wasn't coughing, she was laughing hysterically—she thought our horror show was the funniest thing she had ever seen. It completely ruined the effect. I was so unnerved that I left out eight bars of the Red Death's solo—when she goes around killing everybody—which was just for piano and I knew it by heart and hadn't written it down. She would point at people and they would keel over and die. They all had to remake the steps right onstage during the performance, and dancers were bumping into one another and some got injured. When we took our bows, Red Death pinched me, hard.

I wrote music for student films and plays in college, and after graduation, when I was starting out as a writer, in order to survive, I worked as the rehearsal pianist for a ballet company, touring with them all over the United States and Europe. Luckily, I never had to play at performances, only rehearsals, so I never had the problem of leaving music out of dancers' solos.

Biography:

Grew up: St. Louis, Missouri

Now lives: Rural Thailand, and Boston, Massachusetts

Random fact: Used to like to cook, but is now spoiled by Thai cooks who prepare five-course meals for him

Selected Bibliography:

Oddballs: Stories
Interstellar Pig
The Boy Who Reversed Himself

MICHAEL W. SMITH
Reading and Relating

My dad was a reader. He used to sit in his chair in front of our big living room window and read after dinner. Sometimes I'd sit at the other chair and read as well. We didn't talk much, but I liked sitting next to him. The summer after eighth grade my dad finished a book, and for the first time slid it across the table that separated our chairs. It was *Manchild in the Promised Land*, Claude Brown's autobiographical account of growing up in Harlem. I remember his saying, "Here, read this. It's something you should know about. Don't tell your mother I gave it to you." I didn't know what he meant at the time, but when I started reading it, I sure did. Brown's growing up in Harlem was way different from what I experienced as a white kid in suburban Chicago. He wrote of the drugs and sex and violence that marked his life, and as I read I wondered why it had to be that way. I think maybe whatever social conscience I have started growing as I read that book.

Reading is, perhaps more than anything else, about relationships. It's about having relationships with characters. And authors. But maybe even more than that, reading is about having relationships with the people around you. This is something I observed again and again when my friend Jeff Wilhelm and I studied the literate lives of boys both in and out of school for our book *"Reading Don't Fix No Chevys": Literacy in the Lives of Young Men*. Listen to Bam, an eleventh-grader, talk about *Of Mice and Men:* "Oh, man. I love that book. I read that book eighth, ninth, tenth, and I have it in eleventh grade. I read it every year." Why? His brother, with whom he lived, gave it to him.

Or consider Mark, who got up early to go on the Internet when his favorite hockey team had a late game so he could see how they did. He wanted to know the score, but what was even more important to him was that his friends at school would expect him to know the score.

Buda read the sports pages so he could talk with his dad and friends about them. Neil made a similar point, though he and his friends talked about books and movies instead of the sports pages.

The point is simply this: If somebody tells you that reading is something you do by yourself, tell them they're wrong.

Biography:

Grew up: Milwaukee and Chicago

Now lives: Just outside Philadelphia

Random fact: Is a sports fiend who roots for the Eagles in football, the Sixers in basketball, and the White Sox in baseball

Selected Bibliography:

"Reading Don't Fix No Chevys": Literacy in the Lives of Young Men with Jeffrey D. Wilhelm

MARK TEAGUE
The Dragon in the Big Glommy Castle

My father was an insurance agent, and he changed jobs fairly often. New job, new stationery. The old stationery came to me. Before long I had reams of the stuff, plus all the pencils that got too short for him to use. These are the essential tools for becoming an author/illustrator.

I loved all adventure stories and considered myself to be something of an action hero. When I wasn't out performing heroic acts, I could often be found at home, translating these dramas into fiction. Here is one such piece.

This is a story about three friends: a frog, a turtle, and a raccoon. They have a pretty good life, other than the fact that they are constantly menaced by an evil dragon with a bad toupee. More than once (four times in a sixteen-page story), they are captured, but each time they manage an ingenious escape (they jump out the castle window into the moat).

It is high adventure all the way, and yet more than thirty years after finishing this story I still haven't found a publisher. It's a tough business. I've begun to think that a title would help, so I'm considering "The Dragon in the Big Glommy Castle." What do you think?

Biography:

Grew up: San Diego, California

Now lives: Coxsackie, New York

Random fact: In first grade ate a live fly to prove to his friends that he was a frog

Selected Bibliography:

The Secret Shortcut

The Flying Dragon Room by Audrey Wood

How Do Dinosaurs Say Good Night? by Jane Yolen

Once upon a time there lived a giant dragon who lived in a big glomny castle on the top of a mountain over looking a small village where at night the dragon would hunt and catch people and other animals

JERRY SPINELLI
Bombs, Girls

They were leaning out of Billy's third-floor window, spitting on people walking below. Billy lived above Say-Mor Fashions. Billy was six. So was Philip.

"Here comes one," said Billy.

"It's a girl," said Philip.

"No kidding."

"You gonna spitbomb a girl?"

Billy pushed Philip. Philip went lurching backward onto his rear end.

"I spitbomb anybody," Billy sneered. He pointed to his mouth. "This is an atomic bomb I got here. It's gonna blow her up."

He reverse-snorted and hockered into the bomb bay. He leaned out as far as he could.

Philip leaned out beside his pal. He whispered, "She stopped."

The girl was directly beneath them, looking in the shop window.

"Look!" Philip pointed, but he was careless. His outthrust hand smacked Billy in the cheek.

Billy swallowed.

Again Billy sent Philip reeling. "Look what you did. Now I gotta reload."

Philip hurried back to the window and pointed, this time more carefully. "Look—you can't see her feet. Her things are sticking out. They're in the way."

Billy shrieked, *"Things!"*

Suddenly, the girl was looking up. She shaded her eyes from the summer sun. She smiled. "Hi, guys. Be careful up there. Don't fall out."

Like two turtles, Billy and Philip pulled back into the room.

"Things?" Billy repeated. "Don't you even know what they're called?"

Philip gave a nervous chuckle. "Sure I know."

"So?"

Philip threw out his jaw and came down hard on the "B"— "They're b-b-boobs."

Billy cranked out a jaw of his own. "And what else?"

Philip was stumped. "Huh?"

Billy sneered. "Melons."

Philip's eyes grew large. "Yeah?"

"Yeah." He poked Philip in the chest. "And gazoombas, too."

Philip felt woozy. He went to the window to see with new eyes the things of three words. The girl was walking away. A tiny voice that only he could hear peeped, *Don't go.* Out loud he said, "I wish I had a sister."

"No, you don't," said Billy.

Philip turned. "I don't?"

"Nah. Girls are dumb. They're always doing dumb stuff. Like that one."

"What did she do?"

"She smiled, dumbo."

"What's wrong with that?" said Philip.

"Because that's all they do. They smile and they're nice when they're not supposed to be. They don't even know when it's war. What else do you wanna know about girls? Ask me. Go ahead."

Philip thought, but he couldn't come up with a question.

Billy laid a hand on Philip's shoulder. "You wanna know the main thing about girls? The main number one thing?"

Philip nodded.

Billy sniffed. "They're weak."

"My mother ain't weak," said Philip.

"Trust me," said Billy. "She's weak. Mothers ain't nothin' but big girls. They don't have muscles like us. If you wanted to, you could beat up your mother."

Philip was horrified. "No way!"

"I ain't sayin' you *should*. Or you *would*. I'm just sayin' you *could. If* you *wanted*."

A picture of himself taking a poke at his mother flashed through Philip's brain. He got the chills. "I'm hungry," he said.

"I ain't," said Billy. He spied his plastic weapons on the floor—a rocket launcher and a submachine gun. "Hey!" He tossed Philip the machine gun and kept the rocket launcher for himself.

He pointed out the window, across the street to Rosie's Deli. "Look! A bank! Let's go rob it!"

"All right!" shouted Philip.

They went clattering down the stairs.

Biography:

Grew up: Norristown, Pennsylvania
Now lives: Willistown, Pennsylvania
Random Fact: Has a pet rat

Selected Bibliography:

Maniac Magee
Crash
Wringer

RICK TELANDER

Conduct

It was the end of my sixth-grade year under Miss Lillian Johnson at Kellar Grade School in Peoria, Illinois, more than forty years ago. And something about me, the teacher, the school system— or possibly all three—was way out of whack.

I remember it like it was yesterday. I can see it in the insanity of my old report card, which I have had enlarged and keep in my office desk drawer so that I can occasionally take it out and study it and try not to barf.

I got an A or A-minus for my final grade in eight subjects and a B-plus in science (though I think I got rooked there, since if you add up the six earlier marks, they come out to an A-minus average, but oh well). Then there's my conduct grade. We had As, Bs, Cs, and Ds. But we didn't have Fs. Instead, we had Es. An E was the lowest form of humiliation. And I didn't just have an E in conduct. I had a red E-minus. After that I think came public flogging.

Things hadn't been going well in my arena for much of sixth grade. Or fifth or fourth or third grade, for that matter. In second grade I'd been forced to attend a couple of upsetting parent-teacher conferences. And I'd been sent to the principal's office in first grade for drawing an obscene picture.

Seventh grade was troubling, too, as was eighth. But let's stick with sixth grade. How do you get an A in writing, spelling, reading, English, history, geography, math, and health . . . and a red E-minus in conduct?

Boredom, for one thing. Restlessness, for another. Rebelliousness, for another. Budding hormones for yet another. A keen sense of the absurd. Wiseguy-ism. Blabbering. Access to funny toys.

Indeed, the set of wind-up yakety-yak teeth I'd bought at a mall magic store were angrily taken from me by Miss Johnson one day and stowed in her huge desk drawer. Then they went off. Gee, that was funny! But it didn't help my conduct grade.

There was a kind of consistency to my badness, too. Even before the red E-minus, I'd gotten a C, a C-plus, two C-minuses, and—hello—a red D-minus.

This is what Miss Johnson wrote. First six-week period: "Music grade low because of conduct. Talks—Talks, Talks." Second: "Conduct in class is inexcusable." Third: "Rick is satisfied with less than his best." Fourth: "Improving—but wish he would develop a little more 'Common Sense.'" There was nothing written for the fifth grading period, maybe because I had soared all the way to a C-plus in behavior.

Then came the nuclear explosion. "I hope I am not too much of an 'old crab' to appreciate Rick's brand of humor," wrote Miss Johnson in her notorious red ink for her final, furious assessment. "Maybe I too should stoop so low. That will be the day."

All I had done (among a few other things in the previous weeks) was put a very realistic rubber dog load on her stack of graded papers. (It was that magic store, again. Not me, really.) Miss Johnson passed me, though. Everyone survived. But even now, I'm telling you, the smell lingers.

Biography:

Grew up: Peoria, Illinois
Now lives: Chicago, Illinois
Random fact: Never ate green vegetables (except celery) until age twenty-five

Selected Bibliography:

Heaven Is a Playground
String Music
Heading Home

SCHOLASTIC GROWTH — *Rick T.*

Six Weeks Periods		1st	2nd	3rd	4th	5th	6th	Yr. Ave.
Language Arts	Writing	A-	A	A	A	A	A	A
	Spelling	A	A	A	A	A	A	A
	Reading	A-	B	A-	A	B	A	A-
	English	A-	A	A-	A-	A-	A-	A-
Social Studies	History	B+	A-	B+	A-	A-	A	A-
	Civics							
	Geography	A-	B+	A-	A-	A-	B+	A-
	Arithmetic	A	A	B	B+	A-	B+	A-
	Health	A-	A-	A-		A-	A-	A-
	Physical Ed.							
	Science	A	A	B	B+	A-	B+	B+
Fine Arts	Music	3	2	2	2	2	2	2
	Art	3	2	2	2+	2+	2	2
Days of School		31	31	28	30	30	29	177
Days Absent		1	3	0	0	0	0	4
Times Tardy		0	0	0	0	0	0	0

SOCIAL GROWTH

	1st	2nd	3rd	4th	5th	6th
Conduct	C	D-	C-	C-	C+	E-
Interest in school work						
Attention in class						
Proper use of time	✓	✓	✓			
Effort - Desire to improve						
Courtesy to those in authority						
Respect for regulations						
Consideration of rights of others						
Respect for own and school property						

Conduct grade based on above items. A check mark indicates where improvement is needed.

Scholastic Growth is Graded as Follows:

A	B	C	D	E
94-100	86-93	76-85	70-75	Below 70
Superior	Very Good	Acceptable	Poor	Unsatisfactory

Teacher's Comments

1. Music grade low because of Conduct. Talks - Talks, Talks.
2. Conduct in class is inexcusable.
3. Rick is satisfied with less than his best
4. Improving - but wish he would develope a little more "Common Sense". I hope I am not too much of an "Old Crab" to appreciate Rick's brand of humor. Maybe I too should stoop so low. That will be the day

NED VIZZINI

The Fire Escape

From first grade to fifth grade, I had three best friends: Mark, Randy, and George. They took a year to warm up to me, as if I were an ugly girl, but from then on we were Mark-Ned-Randy-and-George, ready for anything.

One day when we were in second grade, we were sitting in my room looking for trouble when I spotted the big blue extension cord that powered my desk lamp. It was like I was seeing it for the first time.

"Let's climb the fire escape!" I said.

We unanimously decided that this was a good idea. We carried the coiled-up extension cord into the alley behind my house, the one with the dilapidated kiddie pool and cat smell.

The bottom rung of the fire escape ladder hung eight feet off the ground.

I started pitching the extension cord. It took me a good half hour to throw an arced pitch—a swoosh—that threaded the bottom rungs of the ladder and cascaded to the ground right in front of George.

"Awesome!" he said.

"What do we do now?" Mark said.

"We have to make a really good knot," I said.

Mark climbed first. He grabbed the knotted cord and put his

feet on the brick wall of my building. None of us held our breath; there was no question that this would work. He scaled the eight feet slowly, perpendicular to the concrete, drawing the cord taut and then grabbing the bottom rung of the ladder. We all cheered.

Mark clambered up. Mark would go on to be the first person I ever saw smoke pot, in seventh grade, out the window of his living room while his parents were away.

George was next. He climbed flawlessly and silently. He would go on to screw up high school, teach English in Japan, and return to Brooklyn to bartend. This was one of the last years I would see him with his hair short.

Randy followed. He loved the WWF and started his own wrestling league with the toys his parents lavished on him. He now works for the WWF.

Once we got up on the fire escape, we had nothing to do. It was like we'd just climbed Everest; we kind of looked at one another stupidly and then went down, except for Randy: he freaked out and wouldn't leave, so we had to call his mom. She came by to see her second-grader up a fire escape and screamed at us as Randy made tentative plans to jump into her arms. She put the word out to *our* moms and that was it; yelling and punishment ensued. My power cord was taken away and replaced with a thinner one that was thought to be less tempting.

Biography:

Grew up: Brooklyn, New York

Now lives: Brooklyn, New York

Random fact: Thinks one day there really could be a pill to make you cool

Selected Bibliography:

Be More Chill: A Novel

Teen Angst? Naaah . . . A Quasi-Autobiography

CHRIS VAN ALLSBURG

My First Step to the White House

When I was about nine years old, my father bought me a go-kart. It was fire-engine red and had a chain-saw motor on the back that was a screaming terror.

My family lived in a neighborhood where there were winding dirt roads, and it wasn't long before I was blasting through turns sideways, kicking up a rooster tail of gravel.

The roads weren't the only thing that was dirt. So were the driveways. But one morning an asphalt truck pulled up to our house, and by the afternoon our dusty, rutted drive had been transformed into a ribbon of smooth black perfection, the envy of the neighborhood.

A few days later my mom and dad had to go out for the afternoon. Before they left, my dad reminded me of an agreement that we'd made: I would never, ever, use the kart if he wasn't around. If I did, no more go-kart.

After my parents left, my friend Steve came over. One thing led to another, and pretty soon we were rolling the kart out of the drive. I figured one little ride wouldn't hurt. Besides, my dad would never know.

I checked the gas tank on the kart. Empty. We kept the extra gas in a giant ten-gallon army surplus gas can. Steve and I dragged the full can across the driveway and lifted it up. Unfortunately, it was too heavy for us. We ended up pouring one gallon into the cart and about nine gallons onto the driveway.

Do you know what happens to fresh asphalt when gasoline gets on it? Neither did I. It turns into a gooey black muck and sort of melts away. Steve and I stared at the crater in my driveway like it was a chemistry experiment gone very wrong.

I knew I was in big trouble. Not only had I broken my promise about not using the go-kart, I'd also messed up our brand-new driveway. I felt so bad; I just rolled the kart back into the garage.

I waited for my parents to come home, feeling worse every minute. Finally, they pulled into the driveway and parked right over the hole. They hadn't noticed it. Was I lucky!

I knew when my dad discovered the hole, he'd ask me about it. I'd just blame it on the car. Everybody knows cars leak gas, right?

My mom fixed dinner, but I didn't have much of an appetite. In fact, I was starting to feel pretty bad. The idea of waiting until someone discovered the hole and then lying about it was too much for me. I couldn't take it. Before we had dessert, I dragged my dad out to the driveway and confessed. I think I may have started crying a little bit, too. My dad moved the car and looked at the hole. "Well," he said, "that's not too bad. Let's go back in and have some ice cream."

My dad did end up taking the kart away, but only for a few weeks. When I went to my room that night I felt pretty lucky.

Lying in bed, I realized I'd heard about this sort of thing happening before. I'm sure you have heard the story, too. It's called "Parson Weems' Fable," and it tells how young George Washington cut down a cherry tree. When his father discovered the fallen tree, George said, "I cannot tell a lie, Father, I did it with my little hatchet."

George escaped the worse punishment he might have gotten, because he'd told the truth. "Golly," I thought, "I just did that myself!" I fell asleep wondering if one day I'd be president, too.

Biography:

Grew up: Grand Rapids, Michigan

Now lives: Providence, Rhode Island

Random fact: Used to help his dad work his dairy farm. Has seen men in rubber boots shoveling cottage cheese.

Selected Bibliography:

Jumanji
The Mysteries of Harris Burdick
Bad Day at Riverbend

BILL VLASIC
Give a Guy a Newspaper

Guys read newspapers.

Stock tables. Box scores. Movie reviews. Long, detailed stories on conflicts in the Middle East. Short, one-paragraph briefs on bus plunges in Mexico.

It dawned on me growing up in a Detroit suburb, watching my businessman father buried in the morning paper at breakfast—then reading the evening edition with the same scary focus at night. What in blazes could hold his attention like that?

But when I grabbed my first sports section as a second-grader, the mystery was over. There it was, an inning-by-inning account of the game our beloved Tigers had played the night before. Amazing stuff, fresher than my own memory, with pictures and stats and schedules and quirky minutiae. Coolest of all, it was different . . . every . . . *day*.

Before long, my dad noticed me checking him out, like a drooling dog waiting for a scrap off the table. So he'd nonchalantly ask, "Want the sports?" *Uh, yeah, sure, I'll take a look.* Then I'd stick it in my schoolbag and read it later when the nuns weren't looking.

Sports led to comics, then to the TV guide, then into the heavy ink of the news pages. It seemed the paper knew everything, like the weather before it happened. I was on the buffet line of information, chewing up gruesome crime stories and exotic tales of foreign wars. And what about those interesting ads for bras and bikinis? Such a world we lived in!

But mostly I loved the sports page, the ESPN of a kid's imagination in the 1960s. When our local newspapers went on strike during the Tigers' pennant run in 1967, I was outraged. Hey newspaper guys, this is too important to screw around with! My dad was pretty pissed, too.

Giving a guy a newspaper is like teaching him to fish. If he knows where to look, the catch is there. Funny-guy columnist? Check the back page. Weird horoscopes and puzzles? Head off to Features. Tiny little lists of "transactions" involving obscure Triple-A ballplayers? If it isn't in Sports, then it really doesn't matter.

A paper under a guy's arm is insurance against boredom, a companion at the lunch counter, a defense against unwanted conversation on the subway. For a couple of quarters, a guy can surf the news of the world, or just catch up on the shenanigans of the local school board.

I've learned a bit more about how newspapers work in my twenty-six years as a reporter. That pristine morning copy is—too often—the result of a mad scramble for information on deadline the night before. But there's still a mystique to a good newspaper, and a sublime power to educate and inform readers. Kids ask me, "What do you do?" I throw it back. What do you like? Sports? It's in the paper. Politics? Read all about it. Cars, movies, hip-hop? If it's happening, it's there in black and white—and read all over.

One Sunday morning, as I lingered over the NBA standings or some such crucial info, I had that funny feeling of being watched. A certain teenage son of mine had that drooling-dog thing going on.

Uh, want the sports, dude?

Biography:

Grew up: Near Detroit, Michigan

Now lives: Outside Detroit, Michigan

Random fact: Has shaken hands with Larry Bird, George W. Bush, and Robert Goulet

Selected Bibliography:

Taken for a Ride: How Daimler-Benz Drove Off with Chrysler with Bradley A. Stertz

RICH WALLACE
Eat Dirt

This goes back to seventh-grade football. I was one of the small-est guys on the team, but our town revered the game. Even those of us who weren't particularly well suited to be football players went out for a chance to play under the lights in front of thou-sands of people. Soccer was not even an afterthought in that region of New Jersey back in the late sixties.

So I suited up with everybody else, worked my butt off every day, did the drills and took my hits and ran the sprints and came home exhausted and dehydrated every night.

In late August we have our first scrimmage. Hoboken comes to our grassless practice field. They're good and they're big. I don't expect to play much, but I do expect to play.

An hour goes by. They're pounding us on offense and defense. I kneel there with the other scrubs, aching to get in.

Another half hour. Only two or three of us still have clean uniforms. I'm seething—glaring at the head coach through my facemask.

A few more plays. An assistant coach walks over, taps me on the helmet. "Next play, get in there at middle linebacker."

I stand up and put in my mouth guard.

The play ends. I run onto the field. The quarterback does an end-around and I take off in pursuit, but I get cut down by a line-man and wind up eating dirt.

I get to my feet and look around. My teammates are already running toward the goalposts at the other end of the field. "Five laps!" says the coach. "Let's go!"

I stand there dumbfounded. One play? Man, was I pissed off.

So I start sprinting and quickly pass everybody else. They're more tired than I am. They played. I keep sprinting and finish about a lap ahead of the next runner. The head coach looks at me and grins. "You should run cross country in high school," he says.

"I'm not in high school," I say, not bothering to hide my anger.

I think I made my point. The next day he put me on the kick-off team. I played a fair amount that season, even carried the ball a few times. The next year I did better.

In high school, I switched to cross country.

Biography:

Grew up: Hasbrouck Heights, New Jersey

Now lives: Honesdale, Pennsylvania

Random fact: Once wet his pants in a Little League game during a particularly long inning in right field

Selected Bibliography:

Restless: A Ghost's Story

Wrestling Sturbridge

The Roar of the Crowd (Winning Season #1)

WILL WEAVER

Training the Bear

Everybody warns you about drugs. Don't use. Don't carry. However, there's one drug you can't "Just say no" to. In fact, if you're a guy you're carrying it right now. I'm talking about the drug—chemical, actually—testosterone. Testosterone occurs naturally in your body, and it's what physically makes you a man. Testosterone can also make you totally nuts (if you get my pun).

Depending on your age, say twelve or under, you might not be feeling it yet. Like a hibernating bear, your testosterone is still asleep in your muscles, your bloodstream, your glands. In fact, let's call it the Bear. When the Bear wakes, believe me, you'll know it: it will rear up, flex its muscles, and let out a giant roar.

Don't be afraid of the Bear. It's great to suddenly grow hair on your chin, in your armpits, and on your balls (chest hair comes last, by the way). A bear has big bones and muscles, and suddenly yours will grow, too. That's the best part of testosterone.

However, there's also the crazy part—what it does to your

brain. You used to be this nice young boy happy to hang around with your pals. Now you find yourself picking fights with them, or avoiding the losers altogether. Or you're sitting in class doing boring math and suddenly you have a giant tent in your lap. Or you start saying things to girls like, "Hey, Lateesha! Watch me hit my head on my locker—it doesn't hurt!" Or "Hey, Jennifer, I'm going to jump off the roof of my house after school—wanna come watch?" That's not really you talking. That's the Bear.

So what you have to do is get to know your Bear. Try to train him. Make him obey as best you can. This is not easy—especially when he wakes up for the first time and is crashing around the forest, roaring and knocking down trees.

One way to tame your Bear is to get plenty of exercise. Run, shoot hoops, skateboard—whatever—until you're butt-dragging tired. This will take the edge off your Bear. Drink lots of water. Eat right, which means staying off fast food and soda pop—especially Mountain Dew, which has a lot of sugar and caffeine that only makes the Bear wilder (plus rots your teeth). But you can never tame the Bear completely. Wild animal trainers know that. Just when you think your Bear is under control, he will rear up and take a bite out of you.

I'm a fit older guy with mostly gray hair. I have a lovely, classy wife whom I married in college. She's a great woman and I love her. The other day she and I are walking down the street, when another beautiful classy woman passes and gives me a brief smile. Suddenly, my Bear growls. I want to dump my wife, go back to the forest, claw trees, and have bear cubs with this other woman—whom I don't even know!

I mutter something to myself.

"Excuse me?" my wife says pleasantly.

"Just talking to the Bear," I say.

She smiles and holds my arm a little tighter. She knows about the Bear. And now so do you.

Biography:

Grew up: On a dairy farm in northern Minnesota

Now lives: On the Mississippi River in northern Minnesota

Random fact: Owns a dozen hunting guns, but over five hundred books

Selected Bibliography:

Memory Boy

Striking Out

Farm Team

JEFFREY D. WILHELM
Pals Forever: Me, Bobby Fisher, and the Hardy Boys

My old middle school pal Bobby Fisher e-mailed me the other day. I hadn't heard from him in probably thirty years. We were in Webelos and Boy Scouts together; played on the same Little League team (morbidly enough, the Burmeister Funeral Home Bears); and shared many adventures like bike trips, building forts, and playing middle school sports. He'd found a script about a Hardy Boys adventure that we had written and performed in fifth grade as a kind of dress-up book report. Then he'd found my contact information on the Internet and gotten in touch.

As I read his e-mail, memories broke over my consciousness like a warm ocean wave.

My father and mother were teachers, and they didn't consider me much of a reader. They hassled me sometimes because they felt I preferred playing backyard football and basketball to reading or practicing piano. And yet, in my memory, I was always reading. I remember scouring the sports section with Bobby each Saturday and re-enacting "Sudden Sam" McDowell's bid for a no-hitter or a Cleveland Browns game against the archrival Cincinnati Bengals.

I had a complete collection of the old leather-bound Hardy Boys books (I was incredulous years later when my mother gave the whole set away. I'd still love to get them back). Bobby and I read them all, and not just once. Some new mysteries came out when we were in middle school and we read those, too, though we agreed they weren't as good as the old ones. We kept journals and charts to keep track of how Joe, Frank, and Chet solved various mysteries. My old elementary notebooks are also filled with statistics of our baseball team and even neighborhood basketball games.

In fourth grade, our teacher, Miss Burke, challenged us to read one book a day, whatever we chose, and we took it on. We stuck mainly to nonfiction and biographies like those of the mountain man Jim Bridger or historical figures like Abe Lincoln. At the end of the year, Bobby and I each had read 180 books. Nobody else in the class broke one hundred as I remember, and we were mighty proud of ourselves. Each day, I loved changing the number of books I had read under the school photo of myself Miss Burke had hung on the bulletin board.

Through middle school, our friends Bret Bartolovich and Bob Walski joined us in creating an underground newspaper: the *I'll-be-quirky Gay-zette*, which spoofed classroom events and made fun of our teachers, but mostly featured articles of us making fun of one another. When Bobby e-mailed me, I dug some of those old purple manuscripts out. I remember my father mimeographing them at school at our insistence, so we could give them to all our friends. The articles still made me laugh, and through the rough humor, our affection for one another was obvious.

It was impossible not to smile and take a deep breath.

The nostalgia was twofold: for my boyhood, but also for the experiences of the boys I studied with Michael Smith in our *"Reading Don't Fix No Chevys"* project, in which we explored what and how boys really read.

As with the informants we studied in 2000, in the 1960s most of my reading and writing was not school sanctioned but was "underground." I liked to read nonfiction and formula fiction. I privileged humor and edginess. I liked to get a quick sense of accomplishment and to be able to talk with my friends about what I read. I wanted a choice about what to read and write. I liked to write to keep track of characters and of my own achievements in basketball or baseball. From fourth grade to this day, I still keep track of every book I read.

But most of all I'm impressed with the intense social value of literacy. For me, like the boys in our study, reading and writing were not things to do by yourself. Reading was a way of relating to characters, and of imagining we could live through their experiences. But even more importantly, reading and writing were—and still are—ways of sharing and pursuing relationships with my friends. Writing was a way of having fun, and making fun, of one another; of marking our identities as athletes, history buffs, and rebels; and of showing group membership—of proclaiming we were connected to one another.

I'm glad my old friend Bobby e-mailed. It was great to hear from him. And I can't wait to send him a back copy of the *I'll-be-quirky Gay-zette*. Too bad you can't send old mimeographs as an e-mail attachment. Which reminds me that some things about literacy *have* changed, even if our basic experiences of it and motivations for practicing it have not!

Biography:

Grew up: Avon and Amherst, Ohio

Now lives: Boise, Idaho

Random fact: Is a whitewater kayaker and just did Hells Canyon. Eats anchovies on his pizza.

Selected Bibliography:

"Reading Don't Fix No Chevys": *Literacy in the Lives of Young Men* with Michael W. Smith

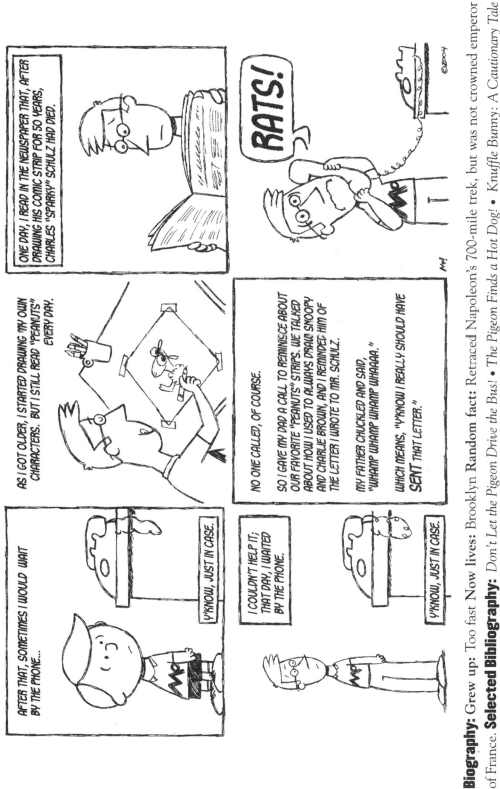

Biography: Grew up: Too fast Now lives: Brooklyn Random fact: Retraced Napoleon's 700-mile trek, but was not crowned emperor of France. **Selected Bibliography:** *Don't Let the Pigeon Drive the Bus!* • *The Pigeon Finds a Hot Dog!* • *Knuffle Bunny: A Cautionary Tale*

LAURENCE YEP

"Puzzle Pieces"
from The Lost Garden

St. Ignatius was a boys' high school founded in 1855, which made it old for San Francisco. It was a hulking three-story stone building that sat on the Stanyan Street hill. Down the slope lay the Haight-Ashbury, where flower power was being born in places like the coffeehouse called The Blue Unicorn. But behind our high school's stone walls we were sheltered from most of those changes.

Our school was blessed with excellent English teachers. In my senior year we had Father Becker, who taught us English by having us imitate various writers and various forms. We had to write poems in the complicated rhyme scheme of the sestina, and we had to write scenes imitating Shakespeare. Our writing would never make anyone forget William or the other greats of English literature, but we learned the nuts and bolts of style. To this day, I have to be careful what I read, because I tend to imitate that writing.

Early in the semester, Father took some of us aside and said that if we wanted to get an A in his course, we would have to get something accepted by a national magazine. All of us were intimidated by the prospect, but in those days you didn't argue with a Jesuit priest—and you still don't. All of us tried. None of us got anything accepted, and he later retracted the threat and graded us by the same standards he used for the rest of the class. However, I got bitten by the bug and kept on trying.

I found that making up my own stories became as much fun

as making explosives. Writing did not make a lightbulb appear over my head. It did not make me scribble away in a frenzy as if I had just been zapped by an electric cattle prod. Nor was it a religious ecstasy. No symphony of cymbals crashed in climax when I reached the final paragraph.

Something else happened instead. Almost everyone I knew—whether they were white, yellow, or black—came from a single background. They were cut from one pattern of cloth. However, I was a bunch of different pieces that had been dumped together in a box by sheer circumstance.

I was a Chinese American raised in a black neighborhood, a child who had been too American to fit into Chinatown and too Chinese to fit in elsewhere. I was the clumsy son of the athletic family, the grandson of a Chinese grandmother who spoke more of West Virginia than of China.

When I wrote, I went from being a puzzle to a puzzle solver. I could reach into the box of rags that was my soul and begin stitching them together. Moreover, I could try out different combinations to see which one pleased me the most. I could take these different elements, each of which belonged to something else, and dip them into my imagination, where they were melted down and cast into new shapes so that they became uniquely mine.

Biography:

Grew up: San Francisco, California

Now lives: Pacific Grove, California

Random fact: At eighteen, published first story in a science fiction magazine . . . for a penny a word

Selected Bibliography:

Dragonwings
Dragon's Gate
Cockroach Cooties

DAVID YOO

Heartbeat

My nickname's "Heartbeat," because my friends swear that you can actually see the pulse on my bare chest. I've always been skinny. Everyone assumes I'm a weakling because I'm so thin (I prefer "lean and mean" or "wiry"), despite being a three-sport athlete. I decided to do something about it this fall when Sarah, the girl I have a crush on, said, "Oh my God . . . you are so skinny." She was visibly repulsed by my sunken chest as I stepped off the soccer bus after practice. I silently vowed to do everything within my power to become the "after" picture. I was sixteen years old, but looked like I was eleven.

For the rest of fall, I did countless push-ups and curled free weights until I couldn't bend my arms. I got ridiculously strong and defined, but I wasn't gaining weight. I wanted to be *thicker*. I didn't care about getting stronger if nobody could tell. I did research, and started lifting heavier weights at lower reps and supplemented my meals with weight-gainer shakes, egg whites, boiled yams, and tubs of cottage cheese. I forced myself to swallow the daily caloric intake equivalent of three overweight men and still wasn't able to increase my mass. (I have a ridiculously fast metabolism.) Over Christmas break I cut out all useless movement, like Ping-Pong and staircases because I'm like a sieve—the 83 calories in a mini-Snickers bar is moot because I waste 90 chewing it.

I returned to school in January depressed, because I was still Heartbeat in everyone's eyes. I constantly weighed myself. At least once an hour, no matter where I was, I'd find a bathroom so I could take off my shirt and flex in the mirror for a couple of minutes. I was so frustrated that nothing was working—but the frustration didn't last. I was sitting in study hall two weeks ago when Sarah said the magic words: "Have you been working out, Dave? You look bigger." I couldn't tell if she was being sarcastic. I went home and inspected myself in the mirror. I did look bigger! But then I realized the reason: I'd accidentally worn *two* T-shirts under my rugby shirt that day. It was just an illusion. I was futilely stuffing my face and religiously pumping iron and failing to alter my appearance, and now I'd stumbled on the simplest solution to looking bigger. I felt like I was reborn.

I went to school the next day wearing two T-shirts under my turtleneck. I felt solid. By the end of last week, I was wearing three T-shirts under my rugby shirt. This Monday I tucked four T-shirts under my plaid button-down. It gave me traps that didn't exist. My Q-tip–sized shoulders transformed into NBA-grapefruit deltoids. I could tell my classmates subtly regarded me differently. It was respect. Sarah gave me a look I'd never seen before, as if she felt . . . *safer* around me. I was walking down the hallway at the end of the day and must have twisted awkwardly because suddenly my zipper literally exploded, and all my T-shirts spilled out of my pants. Luckily, the hallway was empty and I was wearing a belt.

I realized I had artificially outgrown my clothes. My button-downs were so tight that a few seconds after jamming the extra layers into my pants, the pressure would suddenly bunch the cloth up in random places so it looked like I had a goiter on my shoulder or something. I complained to my parents over dinner last night. "I don't fit into anything anymore," I said. "It reflects poorly on you guys. You could get arrested."

"What are you talking about? You look the same as always. You're still my little boy," my dad replied, putting me in a headlock and giving me a noogie. I glared at him.

"I need a new ski jacket," I said. It was true. I could barely clap my hands with all the layers I was wearing. I was getting out of control at this point. The four T-shirts under my wool sweater were smushing my lungs together like a male girdle. It was a small price to pay; nobody called me Heartbeat anymore, I reminded myself.

After dinner I went to a party. Even though it was winter, I opted to hang out on the back porch with the smokers as much as possible because it was so hot inside. Being indoors was like a sauna, but Sarah was in the basement so I headed that way. We were talking and she noticed that I was dripping with perspiration. "You're trembling," she said, touching my shoulder. She thought I was nervous talking to her and probably thought it was cute, but in reality I was on the verge of passing out because I was wearing four tight T-shirts and two long-sleeves under my wool sweater, not to mention the sweatpants tucked into my tube socks to add heft to my (formerly chicken-legs) quads. She squeezed my biceps.

"Jeez, Dave, how many layers are you wearing?"

I couldn't even feel her squeezing them.

"I have to go," I said, excusing myself to another corner of the basement. Everyone was smushed together. It was so hot everyone except me was hanging out in T-shirts and tank tops. I was sopping and delirious and felt claustrophobic. My chest was cold because I had four drenched T-shirts underneath my sweater. It looked like I was breaking out with Ebola or something. When I coughed people turned away from me in fear. *Abandon ship, abandon ship!* I had no choice but to take some layers off. I lurched to the bathroom. My arms were ponderously heavy as I pulled off the sweater. Just lifting my arms exhausted me, and I had to stop midway and take a rest by sitting on the edge of the tub, gasping. I slowly peeled off the layers, one at a time. I took off my pants and peeled off my sweatpants, too, down to my undies. I dried myself off with a wash cloth. My red T-shirt had bled onto the three white Ts because of the sweat, so they now were faded pink tie-dyes. I hoisted the bundle of clothes and was shocked at the weight. I jammed them into the closet. I'd retrieve them later, before I left.

I put my sweater back on without anything underneath. After two weeks of constricting my air supply and range of motion by wearing upwards of six layers, I was amazed at how much freedom I had with my arms. I felt like dancing for the first time in my life. I suddenly realized what I really looked like at this party: a padded, miserable, and frustrated puffball, burning up in all my layers. All this because I hated my nickname?

I got home and realized I'd left my bundle of wet clothes back at the party. I took this as a sign. My days of wearing extra layers was officially over. Had Sarah fallen for the padded me, she'd be falling for someone else. Besides, winter wasn't going to last forever, and I couldn't just revert back to wearing just one set of clothes like a normal human being come spring. The change in my outward appearance would be the equivalent of a sheared sheep. From now on, I was going to just be me.

That was last night. *I'm not disgustingly thin*, I constantly remind myself. I am wiry. I'm lean and mean. Outside it's snowing again. There's a party tonight, and my friends are on their way to pick me up. I don't know what to wear, so I lay out four different outfits on the floor as if they're chalk outlines of people. A car horn honks ten minutes later and I still haven't decided on an outfit. Maybe I'll just wear all of them.

Biography:

Grew up: Avon, Connecticut

Now lives: Boston, Massachusetts

Random fact: Has been wearing the same pair of disposable contact lenses for well over two years

Selected Bibliography:

Girls for Breakfast (available Spring 2005)

PAUL O. ZELINSKY
I Was Young in the Old Days

I was young in the old days. Of course they weren't old days at the time; they were brand-new, just like the days today. My old days go back before homework was discovered, or at least before homework became a major grown-up strategy to keep you from spending your time sitting inside and staring at a TV screen. Then again, in those days, there was nothing on TV. So when you weren't in school, you had more time to pass, and it was up to you to find ways to pass it.

I chose to spend my time sitting inside staring at pieces of white paper. Then I would draw things on them. I had stacks of white paper that were the backs of the extra tests and homework sheets my father would bring home from work (he taught math). I would pull things out of the air and put them on paper, whatever amused me. The crazier the better, was my standard. The main point was to amuse myself. It didn't hurt if other people liked my drawings, too.

It's interesting that what impresses people most is a drawing that looks like real life, yet it's much more natural to learn to draw from other drawings than from looking at real life. I think that's why many kids learn so much about drawing by copying cartoons. I was so excited when my friend Michael Thomas

Paul O. Zelinsky, *age ten*

Paul O. Zelinsky, *2005*

showed me how to draw Fred Flintsone that I still remember, forty-two years later, where we were standing in the school playground at recess that day in fourth grade. I also remember how to draw a pretty fair Fred Flintstone.

I don't remember making the top drawing on the previous page, but my mother wrote a date on it before putting it in a drawer, so I can tell you that I had just turned ten when I drew it. Looking at it now, I think it's still pretty funny. If you've seen the fancy paintings I put into books like *Rapunzel* or *Rumpelstiltskin*, you might not expect to see something like this. But if you're familiar with *The Wheels on the Bus*, you might not be so surprised that as a ten-year-old I was as silly as that.

Biography:

Grew up: Wilmette, Illinois
Now lives: Brooklyn, New York
Random fact: Prefers chocolate to liver

Selected Bibliography:

The Wheels on the Bus
Swamp Angel by Anne Isaacs
Rumpelstiltskin